# DATING
# WITHOUT
# FEAR

# DATING
# WITHOUT
# FEAR

Overcome
Social Anxiety
and Connect

THOMAS SMITHYMAN, PhD

**WINDGRAVE**
— P U B L I S H I N G —

Editor: Greg Larson
Book Launch Manager: Jesse Sussman
Photographer: SJ Smith
Cover and Layout by: Cindy Curtis
*Printed in the USA*

ISBN 979-8-8034118-9-5

*First paperback edition May 2022*

*I'd like to thank all the people who've chosen to do their work with me over the last two decades. I appreciate you for being open, authentic, courageous, and for teaching me so much about social anxiety and humanity. I'd also like to thank my loved ones who have helped me in the process of getting this book out. It would not have been possible without you. After all, it was barely possible with you.*

. . .

# Contents

. . .

# Author's Note

If you've picked up this book, I'm guessing this might be true:

You want to date, connect with others, and form satisfying romantic relationships. You know it's one of the most important things in life. But maybe you get nervous in dating situations or around people you find attractive and you can't help but shut down. Or maybe you find excuses and back away to safety, giving up on trying to meet someone, and then feeling regret and loneliness. Maybe you get hit with strong anxiety and worry that people will be able to tell and think badly of you. Perhaps you've dated sometimes, but it's been a while and you have a feeling that your anxiety is holding you back.

It can be so hard to date when your social anxiety gets triggered at every turn. If this sounds like you, you're not alone.

I wrote this book to help you overcome your social anxiety—in dating situations and in life—to form fulfilling, genuine connections that are rooted in authentic self-confidence.

I'm a clinical psychologist and for the last fifteen years I've specialized in helping clients with social anxiety and what I call dating anxiety—social anxiety that becomes particularly activated in dating contexts. I was drawn to this work because of how much social anxiety has affected me personally, in life and particularly in dating. I was driven to find the solutions to the anxiety that plagued me from a young age.

This book is based on a combination of personal experience, working with clients, and tons of published research collected over a twenty-year period. My goal was to make this book as readable as possible, so I didn't include every research article that has impacted me, and I decided against doing academic footnotes or citations throughout the text. However, I've made a concerted effort to acknowledge the work of the researchers who have influenced this book and my understanding of social anxiety.

At the end of each chapter, you'll find a bibliography of articles that were referenced in that chapter. These are arranged under each chapter's subheadings and should give you a good next step if you wish to follow up this text by reading the relevant psychological literature. The researchers and practitioners that have provided the absolute core of my understanding of social anxiety are Paul Gilbert, Stefan Hofmann, David Moscovitch, Adrian Wells, and David Clark.

When referencing research and literature, I describe not necessarily a summary of the researchers' work or their conclusions, but rather how I interpreted what they found. I focus on how these studies impacted my understanding of social anxiety, and the takeaways that have been most resonant and impactful based on my personal experience and work with clients. By its nature, these reflections on the literature are my subjective views—I hope the way they are presented here conveys the significance of this research and the brilliant work of the researchers, and I also encourage you to seek out the referenced articles and studies for additional learning from the primary source.

The events and stories documented in this book happened as best as I can remember. My patient examples are real, though identities have been obscured for confidentiality. I have had very similar conversations with multiple people—there is often commonality to the social anxiety experience—so some information may have been combined or could be ascribed to several people.

While reading, you'll notice that the word "attractive" is used many times. I used the word in the way that I understand it—somebody who attracts you. What attracts us is always individual and subjective. I did not intend the word attractive to describe someone as conventionally good-looking, and certainly not as some indicator of a person's value in society. Instead, the word attractive is used here to describe what attracts us individually, and to emphasize the way social anxiety gets particularly activated in romantic contexts.

Finally, the material in this book applies broadly across gender and sexuality, since social anxiety also applies broadly across gender and sexuality. You will notice that the vast majority of patients I've worked with in treatment are socially anxious men who are interested in dating women, so these perspectives, along with my own personal experience, comprise much of the included stories. Even if this perspective doesn't apply to you, I believe the principles and information will still be relevant.

After reading, I hope you'll have more understanding of your anxiety, how it affects your behavior, and have tools to safely overcome it and form genuine, fulfilling connections with others, in both romantic and social contexts at large.

It's possible to overcome your social anxiety, and it's possible to date without fear. No matter how anxious we find ourselves right now, these are things we can learn.

— Thomas Smithyman, Ph.D.
April 2022

. . .

# The Warm Social World Awaits

I clearly remember the moment I realized I'd over-come my stubborn, infuriating dating anxiety. I was in Harvard Square, and I saw a beautiful woman walking in my direction through the busy thoroughfare.

I didn't look away. I didn't pretend I hadn't noticed her. I didn't pretend I wasn't interested. I didn't even imagine her look of disgust if I tried to talk to her. Instead, in front of an audience of dozens of people enjoying their day, I smiled, walked up to her, and gamely said the first thing that popped into my head.

How did she respond?

She rejected me. She laughed and kept walking like my attempt at connection was a little joke I'd told her as she passed by.

There was a time when that response would have killed me inside. But not in that moment.

See, as far back as I can remember, I was terrified of women.

Not all women, mind you—just the ones I was attracted to. Go figure. I'm not overly anxious in general, either. I have zero issues making friends, and I've always thrived in social networks. But when I saw or met girls I liked, I fell to pieces.

At times my value as a human seemed entirely dependent on how my most recent dating interaction went. In a variety of ways, this problem has dominated my life. Like many others in my profession, you could argue that I became a clinical psychologist in an attempt to understand and solve my own problems. Yeah, that's probably true. But here's where I differ from most clinical psychologists: on top of the fourteen years of rigorous schooling and intense training I went through to earn my Ph.D. and license, I've spent just as much time doing my own unaffiliated, unpublished research.

I've been experimenting—with myself and my clients—trying to solve the problem of dating anxiety. Be forewarned: some of my experiments and suggestions in this book will sound nutty at first, but I promise you two things:

1. Everything I recommend is backed by a combination of extensive scientific research, clinical practice, and personal experience.
2. I'll never recommend anything that's "take cocaine as an over-the-counter painkiller" level crazy.

This book is my attempt to help you overcome dating anxiety, using both the mainstream scientific research I did while earning my Ph.D., and the rogue experiments I do in my personal life and in my clinical practice.

Just so you know, I'm only playing up my unconventional methods to prove a point: any psychologist can read the literature and understand dating anxiety from a theoretical standpoint. Similarly, non-psychologists can try experiments to overcome their dating anxiety.

I attempt to do both: I do the research, and back it up with real-world exercises. This book is my attempt to share the game-changing results I've learned from my experiments so far, so you can understand your anxiety and create more fulfilling connections.

## My Most Dangerous Experiment: Rejection Month

Back to Harvard Square. That interaction was the tail-end of a month-long experiment I called "rejection month."

The rules were simple: every day, I had to go up to the woman I found most attractive and ask her out. Simple? Sure. Easy? Hell. No.

Talking to random girls was the scariest thing I could imagine—a fate my anxious brain treated as akin to death—and yet, by day thirty in Harvard Square, I did it without feeling a hint of nerves. Her rejection bounced off my chest like a bullet off the Man of Steel.

At any point in my life before then, that rejection would have led to crippling shame and a retreat into the corner of my bedroom to drink cheap wine and ruminate on my lonely life. Instead, her rejection billowed me with pride. When she laughed in dismissal of me, I laughed in return, recognizing the memorable moment I found myself in.

I had won. That was the moment I realized I no longer had any dating anxiety. Over the course of a painful month, I had developed a superpower where one of my biggest weaknesses once stood: I could talk to whoever I wanted, whenever I wanted, completely immune to rejection.

I'd like to think I solved it all in a month, but that's not true. It took me decades of painstaking treatment, practice, research, and experimentation to get to that point. But luckily for you, I've gone through the wall first, and I've distilled all of my research and behavioral experiments into this book so you don't have to go through the wringer yourself.

## Loneliness Is Hell

Experiencing social anxiety is an intense form of suffering—and I choose the word "suffering" purposefully.

For example, one of my patients made $500,000 per year.

"But I'd give it all away if someone could relieve my anxiety," he told me.

He eventually progressed so far that he no longer needed treatment. And just so you know, I didn't ask for $500,000 in return. I joke, but the pain of dating anxiety is deadly serious and legitimate.

Connection is one of our most basic human needs, and we suffer intensely without it. Just in case you need more convincing, consider the following:

- Social isolation can be our most intense form of punishment.
- Loneliness is as dangerous for your health as smoking cigarettes.
- A lack of satisfying social connections is one of the main risk factors for suicides and is a strongly-contributing factor in drug problems.

And in one of the most shocking examples I've ever heard, a caller on a dating advice show asked how he could acquire chemical castration to suppress his innate drives and overcome the pain of his unfulfilled sexual desires. I had a client later who asked me the same thing!

With emotional pain so deep that you'd rather castrate yourself than live another day with your unmet needs, it's no wonder if you're angry at yourself (or the whole damn dating world, for that matter).

We've all been there: that painful moment when you get home from the bar, slam the door, then admonish yourself for not having the courage to talk to anyone. This intense regret, suffering, and self-flagellation isn't enough to get us over our fears. We need something more effective...

## The Warm Social World Awaits

Have you ever seen one of those sci-fi shows where people enter a new dimension of their familiar world? Most of the world might look the same, but something fundamental has shifted, so you know it's not the same place. Maybe the people look normal, but the sky is green. Or maybe the landscape looks like Earth, but all the people have permanent smiles on their faces.

That's how socially comfortable people see the world: it looks almost exactly like your "dimension" of the world, but something feels positively different.

That's what I call the Warm Social World. Though socially comfortable people live among us, looking around at the same places and people, what they see and experience is completely different. When they look at others, they see potential friends and connections. They anticipate fun conversations and a chance to improve everyone's day. Their social lives are full, and making friends is easy. By extension, dating is easier for them, too.

Hard to imagine, isn't it? It was for me, too. Believe it or not, that Warm Social World is already all around you. You just need the right tools to see it.

## Seduction Is Overrated

When you're nervous, you don't live in the Warm Social World. You live in the World of Threat, where you can't help but see everything through the lens of anxiety.

Going from the World of Threat to the Warm Social World is difficult. Trust me, I've done it myself. And most of the actions to make that shift are counterintuitive.

In this book, you'll learn the truth behind dating anxiety: that it's a finely-tuned system meant to shut us down and protect ourselves from getting socially injured or rejected.

I'll show you how our protective behaviors actually increase our anxiety:

- If you hide from people, they start to seem scarier.
- If you focus on your inferiority, you become more insecure.
- If you critique your social performance, you feel defeated even before your next interaction.
- If you imagine how others might see you, you become more self-conscious and self-critical.

- If you hide who you are, you reinforce the idea that you're not good enough.

In this book, we'll change all this. We'll break down your protection system until you understand it well enough to overcome it.

However, be warned: this is *not* a book about how to seduce people. You might become a great dater as a result of what I teach you—in fact, it's likely. But, unlike most books on the topic, this isn't a guide for becoming more attractive, earning approval, or winning friends and influencing people. Those are all ideas based on the premise that we solve dating problems from the outside. I firmly believe the best way to enter the Warm Social World is to transform the internal psychological issues that cause your external problems.

> **DISCLAIMER**
>
> Although I will use real clinical examples throughout the book, I've obscured everyone's identities for confidentiality.

## Welcome to Your New Life

I will never advise you to do anything I haven't already done myself. Seriously.

Sure, I've learned immensely from my own experiences, but I've also taken a lot from the deep courage of my clients. In fact, I often do the exercises in this book *with* my clients, so I guess that makes you one of my honorary clients. I've seen the people I work with transform their lives with the tools I'm about to give you. They've done things that felt worse than death. Some have gone from being scared to leave their apartments to establishing real and satisfying relationships. They've built full social lives. Transforming was never easy for them, but it was always worth it, no matter how painful it was in the moment.

I have great respect for anyone who's willing to face their issues and move towards their fear, even when everything inside you screams to stay safe in your comfortable loneliness.

What I'll teach you in this book isn't quick, and it isn't easy. But it's worth it.

Most people never admit their issues. Even fewer confront those issues and try to improve. It's the rare and courageous few who are willing to go through the deeply fulfilling journey of overcoming their anxieties. By reading even this far, you're already part of this psychologically developed and powerful minority. Congratulations. Seriously.

Having said that, your work is just beginning. Let's get started—the first chapter of your new life lies ahead.

# The Warm Social World Awaits

Connection is one of our basic needs
and we suffer intensely without it

Baumeister, R. F., & Leary, M. R. (1995). The need to belong: Desire for interpersonal attachments as a fundamental human motivation. *Psychological Bulletin, 117*(3), 497–529.

Calati, R., Ferrari, C., Brittner, M., Oasi, O., Olié, E., Carvalho, A. F., & Courtet, P. (2019). Suicidal thoughts and behaviors and social isolation: A narrative review of the literature. *Journal of Affective Disorders,* 245, 653–667.

McClelland, H., Evans, J.J., Nowland, R., Ferguson, E., & O'Connor, R. (2020). Loneliness as a predictor of suicidal ideation and behaviour: A systematic review and meta-analysis of prospective studies. *Journal of Affective Disorders, 274*(3), 880-896.

Dush, C.K., & Amato, P. (2005). Consequences of relationship status and quality for subjective well-being. *Journal of Social and Personal Relationships, 22*(5), 607-627.

Cacioppo, J., Hawkley, L., Norman, G., & Berntson, G. (2011). Social isolation. *Annals of the New York Academy of Sciences, 1231*(1), 17-22.

Holt-Lunstad, J., Smith, T. B., & Layton, J. B. (2010). Social relationships and mortality risk: A meta-analytic review. *PLoS medicine, 7*(7), e1000316.

Christie, N. C. (2021). The role of social isolation in opioid addiction. *Social Cognitive and Affective Neuroscience, 16*(7), 645–656.

# CHAPTER 1

. . .

# What Is Dating Anxiety?

"I can't take this anymore," he said. "I'm willing to give your treatment six months. If that doesn't work, I'm going to kill myself."

That's one of the first things my patient Steve said to me. He was a young, smart, athletic guy. He was about to start business school. From the outside, he had everything going for him. But on the inside, he was truly suffering. In his 28 years, Steve had only been in one relationship, which lasted just a few months during his early twenties.

He could hardly stand to be around women he found attractive, let alone be *himself* around them. Instead, he put his energy into "saying the right thing" to women, which never worked. Later he would replay the interactions in his head, again and again, looking for ways to improve, and punishing himself for everything he did wrong. He even beat himself up over interactions he'd had with women more than ten years in the past!

For Steve, dating anxiety had pushed him to the verge of suicide. He's not alone, either. Social isolation and loneliness are some of the biggest risk factors for suicide. Maybe you've felt the same way at some point in your dating life. In this chapter, we'll unmask dating anxiety, break it down to its fundamental characteristics to show you just how common it is, and lay the groundwork for transforming it into something much more beneficial.

## The Real Symptoms of Dating Anxiety

Let's dig deeper into Steve's experiences with dating anxiety to show you the common symptoms:

- Steve started shaking when he interacted with a woman he liked, his voice became high-pitched, and he stumbled over his words.
- When Steve was in the presence of a woman he liked, his brain sensed

a dangerous situation. As such, his body triggered a flood of chemical and hormonal changes to protect him, similar to if he'd encountered a tiger. This led to a faster heart rate, shallow breathing, shaking, and sometimes blushing or sweating.

- He also had some cognitive symptoms. He found it hard to focus or think easily or creatively around women. That meant he was unable to think of something to say.

- Dating anxiety is rarely just simple nerves. Along with intense fear, Steve also experienced strong feelings of shame. This shame led to chronic low moods, anger at the way people treated him, and growing resentment.

- As you can imagine, Steve was also terribly lonely, the negative consequences of which are vastly underestimated (we'll explore this more as the book goes on).

- Steve's biggest problem, and his presenting complaint, was that he avoided social situations where he might encounter people he found attractive. This is very common and leads to the deepest source of suffering in dating anxiety: not developing the relationships you desire.

- Due to intense fear, he stayed away from most social situations. He also avoided young women when he came across them in the course of his day.

- Steve also practiced avoidance in more subtle ways. He protectively shut down his personality in social interactions with women. He didn't make eye contact, he said nothing or as little as possible, and he kept his face tense and emotionless. Though physically present, he was socially inaccessible. He actively tried to prevent others from talking to him by trying to appear busy, serious, or tired. He would do this by pretending to be really engaged in something else, like his phone.

Does any of this sound familiar? Let's talk about it...

## Stuck in a Prison of Your Mind

Though you may not experience the exact same symptoms of dating anxiety as Steve, you almost certainly experience one core problem in dating anxiety:

An unhelpful focus of attention.

Here's what that means: when you're experiencing dating anxiety, your attention—which should be focused on what's happening around you or the person you're talking to—gets pulled into your head. You focus on things that could go wrong, the "stupid" thing you said a minute ago, or you're analyzing what someone thinks of you. It's all devastatingly unhelpful.

When we get stuck in our heads during social interactions, we're not in the moment. We engage in "mindreading," the belief that you can tell what people think about you (and what we imagine they think is almost always negative). We then replay the events endlessly afterward.

> **MINDREADING**
> Mindreading is a sneaky and underrecognized symptom of dating anxiety, and social anxiety in general.

Steve tormented himself with self-criticism and a slew of exaggeratedly negative interpretations of other people's behavior—a look one woman gave him, something a guy at the bar said, or how his Uber driver talked to him—and they all focused on himself, his performance, what he assumed other people thought of him, his history, and his future. He believed he came across to others as weak and childish, and that women would be disgusted if he showed any interest in them. He believed that whatever he said had to be impressive, or girls would be dismissive. If he wasn't able to think of something clever or funny, he would say nothing. Then he would go home and suffer the anger and regret of another social failure.

Is it any wonder he was contemplating suicide? He'd become a prisoner of his own mind.

If you experience something similar, please know this: you're not suffering alone.

## Dating Anxiety is Normal

Steve looked me in the eyes one session and said, "The worst part about all this is that I know it's just me. I look around and I see all these happy, confident people, interacting so easily. What the hell is wrong with me? How come I'm the one feeling like this?"

Despite the empathy I felt for him, I couldn't help but chuckle wryly to myself. I couldn't count how many times I'd felt the same exact things as him, and how many clients and friends I've met who suffered the same way. As a clinical psychologist who specializes in social anxiety, he wasn't even the first person I spoke to *that day* who experienced dating anxiety to the extent he did.

The fact is, dating anxiety is quite common. At least 13% of young people suffer from a significant level of dating anxiety. This shouldn't be surprising given that *social* anxiety—the larger umbrella under which dating anxiety falls—is the fourth most common psychological disorder in the US, believed to currently affect 15 million people in this country alone. This number may even be underestimated, since social anxiety has low rates of self-reporting and people may not recognize their experience as a treatable disorder. Early-stage romantic interactions, such as flirting and first dates, are among the most common trigger situations for social anxiety. In my clinical experience, the three scariest situations for socially anxious people are public speaking, job interviews, and early dating interactions (most likely because these situations inherently involve the risk that others will see and judge our weaknesses).

Dating anxiety is so normal that it's built into our dating customs. We assume that people are anxious when they first meet a potential date, therefore most flirtation demonstrates a mix of anxiety and warmth designed to make other people feel safer and more comfortable.

Despite what you see in movies, most people don't casually saunter up to people at bars and seduce them with confident witticisms. First of all, most of us are far too worried that we'll get rejected. And secondly, a lot of courtship interactions these days happen online through the aid of dating apps. We usually need a lot of encouragement and clear evidence that we'll be accepted before we're willing to risk initiating a conversation with a stranger we're attracted to.

**ANXIETY UNDER IDEAL CONDITIONS**

Guys are far more likely to talk to a warm and smiling woman than someone who appears very physically attractive but cold. But more likely than anything else is talking to nobody at all. In a 2008 French study, male participants encountered a woman who sat alone reading a book in a social environment. The woman made regular and inviting eye contact with the men, but very few initiated a conversation.

> In other words, the vast majority of men will not approach a woman even under ideal conditions.

In college, I worked with a young guy who considered himself a dating failure. In part because he imagined all his classmates were out meeting new people all the time, having endless strings of dating partners, hooking up, and going to movie-style college parties full of sorority models in bikinis. And there he was, sitting alone in his dorm room. The serial daters do exist, but they're outliers—few and far between. We overestimate how socially successful everybody else is, and underestimate how normal our anxieties are.

---

**ARE WE MORE SEXLESS?**

Multiple studies have shown that people are having less sex than our parents and grandparents did. For example, in the last 20 years, the percentage of men who report not having sex has almost doubled. Moreover, over 80% of Americans had 0-1 sexual partner in the previous year. Those who had more than 5 partners— the outliers, not the norm—were only 3.2% of the population.

---

## "Normal" Doesn't Mean Happy

Just because what you're experiencing is common doesn't make it any less painful. Trust me, I've been there. I just don't want you to beat yourself up for experiencing dating anxiety (rather than motivating you, that actually makes it worse).

Though dating apps are marketed as a way to help you find more people in your busy life, I believe they're actually gaining popularity for a different reason: they allow us to avoid the explicit face-to-face rejection and fear of early dating—we swipe a picture from the safety of distance, rather than initiating a conversation and observing the person's response. Of course, the apps don't allow you to completely avoid the risks associated with romantic connection, they just put them off until later.

> Many recent technological advances may be inspired by anxiety avoidance. One opinion piece I read in GQ hypothesized that everything from Uber to GrubHub to Tinder was developed as means to get more done without ever engaging with anybody. The author noted that GrubHub's advertising was the most blatant:
>
> "Everything great about eating, combined with everything great about not talking to people."

Dating anxiety is so common that I encourage you to assume that everybody feels as nervous as you do and act accordingly. In fact, one of my favorite studies (from 1996) found that the majority of people have

failed to pursue a romantic relationship with someone they liked due to fear of rejection. And if you're
thinking, "Well, it's worse for me," the study found
that the majority of people think that too!

## "If Dating Anxiety Is so Common, How Come I Feel so Alone?"

Much of dating anxiety is driven by shame. There's
still a lot of cultural shame around dating anxiety,
plus it's normal to fear that others will think less of
you if they know about your anxiety. So I ask you:

*How many people have you told about your dating
anxiety struggles?*

I'm guessing it's not one of your go-to conversation topics. You'd need to really trust somebody
before you revealed something so vulnerable. Other
people are exactly the same way. People don't tend
to bust out all of their vulnerabilities at the drop of
a hat, especially when they fear rejection.

And yet, shame is best treated by talking about it
(and receiving acceptance and support in response).
Shame can be very damaging, especially since it
encourages us to hide away. This is the fundamental
reason we feel so alone with our anxiety: because
people don't talk about it. We only have access to our
own thoughts and emotions, nobody else's.

That favorite study I just mentioned above was designed by a group of psychologists trying to tackle a fascinating problem: what happens that prevents two single people who are into each other from dating? They found that when we're asked why we didn't make a move or show interest, we point to our fear of rejection as the reason. But if we're asked why we think the other person didn't make a move, we're convinced it's because they weren't interested. Think about that. We assume totally different causes for our inaction because we only have access to our own thoughts and feelings. This is a phenomenon one of my colleagues refers to as "comparing our insides to other people's outsides."

What would happen if we instead assumed everyone was like us: too nervous to take risks and show their interest?

This is a hard pill to swallow because thinking this way forces you to make difficult choices. It's actually easier to assume there's something wrong with you *externally*. But I challenge you to think differently. Buying better clothes, getting in great shape, or learning funny things to say might be helpful at some point. But what if you focused your energy on changing yourself *internally* at first? What if you asked yourself:

*What can I do to fix my pain from the inside out, not the outside in?*

## Dating Anxiety: The Wound Even Time Won't Heal

A sense of belonging is one of our fundamental human needs. If we don't bond with people, we suffer deeply. Romantic relationships are typically where people find their deepest emotional connections, and dating anxiety is a harsh barrier that prevents these needs from being met. I've seen people suffer with dating anxiety in many ways: fear, loneliness, depression, shame, alcoholism, bitterness, and, at the extreme end, suicide.

### HEALTH AND LONELINESS

Our need to belong is so fundamentally important that it even affects our physical health. Loneliness is as bad for us as smoking cigarettes, having high blood pressure, being obese, or not exercising. It even makes us more likely to catch a cold. We need satisfying connections for basic health.

Family relationships and deep friendships are beneficial, but they're not enough—we have a special need for romantic relationships. Studies on well-being consistently find that the further along we are in a positive, committed relationship, the happier and healthier we become.

The problem is that dating anxiety conspires against us on our path to potential relationships, every step of the way. Here's how:

When your threat system is on—that protective mode where you hide from social risks—you're less likely to leave the house or go places where you might meet a potential partner. If by some stroke of luck you do get a date, you'll find it hard to be authentic and, therefore, connect. As such, it's hard to reveal when you like someone when you're feeling anxious, so you don't take the necessary risks to develop your potential relationships. Why? Because each of these moves risks rejection. So despite a mutual interest with someone, you'll still fail to enter the satisfying relationship you crave.

I've even seen dating anxiety get in the way of established relationships, in which somebody is unable to show their true self, so they never feel fully loved. In other words, dating anxiety may not fix itself *even if you enter a relationship.*

This is one wound that even time won't heal; it can only be fixed with action.

## Social Anxiety Is Chronic and Unremitting

Phil, a new patient, came to see me while I was writing this chapter. At our first meeting, he was stiff and uncomfortable but very polite and eager to talk about his problems. I asked him why he chose now to get treatment.

"Well, I've just turned forty and I figured it's time to make a change. I've always had social anxiety, ever since I was a kid. Without noticing, it took up more and more real estate in my life. All my hobbies accommodate my social anxiety, and my work is great for somebody who doesn't want to interact with people. There are only certain areas I'll go to or activities I'll engage in, so my social life is limited to a few close friends. I've only been in a couple of very brief relationships. I just looked around recently and wondered whether my whole life was built to protect me from my social anxiety."

He tried to change things on his own over the years, but we all know how that goes. His actions boiled down to avoiding situations that made him anxious. And sure, when you cope that way, nothing gets so bad that you fall to pieces. But things never get better, either.

He continued: "Now I'm in my forties, and I'm wondering if my life can be more than this. If I don't really give this a shot and try to change now, maybe this is what my life is. I want to try treating it once, for real."

Since that first meeting, Phil has already made tremendous progress because he's chosen to face his problems. Each week, his anxiety drops, he's slowly taking back territory, and his life is getting a little bit better day by day.

Phil's story mirrors much of what I see working with patients. On average, only a minority of people seek treatment for their social anxiety. And it appears the average person waits six to sixteen years before seeking help.

There's even evidence to suggest that social anxiety itself is a barrier to seeking treatment. Admitting you need help can bring up feelings of shame and embarrassment, keeping the very people who need the most help from getting it.

Social anxiety doesn't just go away. Instead, without treatment, it slowly gets worse. There are two reasons for this: one is that getting worse is the natural progression of anxiety, and two is that most dating advice often violates even the most fundamental treatment principles.

Allow me to expand briefly: as we'll discuss in-depth throughout the book, we engage in self-protective behaviors when we're anxious. Research clearly shows that our defensiveness actually feeds anxiety over time—the more you avoid something you're afraid of, the stronger your anxiety about that thing becomes in the long term. Treatment turns this equation on its head. If you drop your self-protection and thoughtfully move towards your fear, you'll break through and reduce your anxiety.

Secondly, people who are anxious about dating are likely to look for advice on the internet, and that advice is often counter-productive. How do I know? Because that's where I went, way back in the late 90s. While I read online dating advice, I felt excited and hopeful. But when I went into social situations armed with that advice, I was often more anxious than ever and less likely to actually talk to anybody.

Unfortunately, a lot of online dating advice you come across violates basic treatment principles and makes your dating anxiety substantially worse. For example, most online dating advice focuses on changing your external performance, thus drawing your attention to yourself and making you more self-conscious. This dating advice misses the fact that increased performance demands and self-focused attention escalate your anxiety.

**UNHELPFUL ONLINE DATING ADVICE**

Here's the most egregious example of anxiety-inducing online dating advice I ever came across: a dating coach who encouraged people to be aware of a list of 25 things they must never do while interacting. The list included things like speaking with a high voice, leaning forward in social settings, and making jokes. No jokes? What a buzz kill!

Additionally, this task is impossible. We can only keep a handful of things in mind at any given moment, and the higher demand we place on ourselves, the more anxiety we feel, and the more anxiety we feel the more likely we are to avoid a situation.

Back when I first read the article, I thought I must be doing at least a dozen things wrong without even realizing it. I was sure I'd been making a terrible impression on everyone I met. I wondered how I'd ever be good enough to socialize again!

## Steve and the Six-Month Deadline

Steve, the patient who said he would give treatment six months before killing himself, kept coming back. Somewhere around that six-month mark, we met for his regularly scheduled session.

He was in a good mood, and he talked excitedly about his most recent date that week. At this point, he was dating regularly, but still on the lookout for the deep relationships that really mattered to him. That day he was buoyant because this most recent date, with a high-spirited college student, was something of a breakthrough.

His homework had been to experiment with dropping his "strong silent type" protective facade, show his real self, and find out whether he was as unappealing as he feared. To his surprise, his results were almost the exact opposite of his expectations. When he allowed himself to be authentic, he found it much easier to think of things to say to his date, and he found that his date became more talkative also. They connected easily, and he allowed his normally-hidden attraction to emerge in a very natural flirtation. The evening blossomed, and he found himself in his first romantic relationship in almost ten years. The relationship was brief, but it was a great start.

You see, when he first came in, it was very important for Steve to learn that dating anxiety is a common experience and that his deep suffering was both legitimate and understandable. But before he could believe things could improve, he had to understand the problem a little more deeply.

Steve's experience, my experience, your experience, and millions of others' experiences all beg the same questions:

*Why is dating anxiety so common?*

*Why are we saddled with something so damaging?*

*If such a great life awaits us on the other side of dating anxiety, why do we have it in the first place?*

After all the pain your anxiety has caused you, you deserve some answers.

# CHAPTER 1 REFERENCES

# What Is Dating Anxiety?

Social isolation and loneliness are linked to suicide

Calati, R., Ferrari, C., Brittner, M., Oasi, O., Olié, E., Carvalho, A. F., & Courtet, P. (2019). Suicidal thoughts and behaviors and social isolation: A narrative review of the literature. *Journal of Affective Disorders, 245*, 653–667.

McClelland, H., Evans, J.J., Nowland, R., Ferguson, E., & O'Connor, R. (2020). Loneliness as a predictor of suicidal ideation and behaviour: A systematic review and meta-analysis of prospective studies. *Journal of Affective Disorders, 274*(3), 880-896.

## The Real Symptoms of Dating Anxiety

A summary of the physiological process of being socially anxious, and why we feel what we feel

Thomas, S. A., Aldao, A., & De Los Reyes, A. (2012). Implementing clinically feasible psychophysiological measures in evidence-based assessments of adolescent social anxiety. *Professional Psychology: Research and Practice, 43*(5), 510–519.

The general symptoms of dating anxiety

Chorney, D.B., & Morris, T. (2008). The changing face of dating anxiety: Issues in assessment with special populations. *Clinical Psychology: Science and Practice, 15*(3), 224-238.

## Dating Anxiety is Normal

Social anxiety and dating anxiety are highly correlated

Robins, C. J. (1986). Sex role perceptions and social anxiety in opposite-sex and same-sex situations. *Sex Roles: A Journal of Research, 14*(7-8), 383–395.

Xu, Y., Schneier, F., Heimberg, R., Princisvalle, K., Liebowitz, M., Wang, S., & Blanco, C. (2012). Gender differences in social anxiety disorder: Results from the national epidemiologic sample on alcohol and related conditions. *Journal of Anxiety Disorders, 26*(1), 12-9.

MacKenzie, M.B., & Fowler, K. (2013). Social anxiety disorder in the Canadian population: Exploring gender differences in sociodemographic profile. *Journal of Anxiety Disorders, 27*(4), 427-34.

## Rates of Dating Anxiety

McNamara, J. R., & Grossman, K. (1991). Initiation of dates and anxiety among college men and women. *Psychological Reports, 69*(1), 252–254.

Chorney, D.B., & Morris, T. (2008). The changing face of dating anxiety: Issues in assessment with special populations. *Clinical Psychology: Science and Practice, 15*(3), 224-238.

Rates of social anxiety
Jefferies, P., & Ungar, M. (2020). Social anxiety in young people: A prevalence study in seven countries. *PloS one, 15*(9), e0239133.

Harvard Medical School, 2007. National Comorbidity Survey (NCS). (2017, August 21).

Kashdan, T. B., & Herbert, J. D. (2001). Social anxiety disorder in childhood and adolescence: Current status and future directions. *Clinical Child and Family Psychology Review, 4*(1), 37–61.

Muzina, D.J., & El-Sayegh, S. (2001). Recognizing and treating social anxiety disorder. *Cleveland Clinic Journal of Medicine, 68*(7), 649-57.

Erwin, B.A., Turk, C.L., Heimberg, R.G., Fresco, D.M., & Hantula, D.A. (2004). The Internet: Home to a severe population of individuals with social anxiety disorder? *Journal of Anxiety Disorders, 18*(5), 629-46.

We overestimate how anxious we are,
and underestimate how anxious others are
White, K., & Van Boven, L. (2012). Immediacy bias in social-
emotional comparisons. *Emotion, 12*(4), 737–747.

Thibodeau, M., Gómez-Pérez, L., & Asmundson, G.J. (2012).
Objective and perceived arousal during performance
of tasks with elements of social threat: The influence
of anxiety sensitivity. *Journal of Behavior Therapy and
Experimental Psychiatry, 43*(3), 967-74.

## Anxiety Under Ideal Conditions

Guys are more likely to talk to a smiling woman
Moore, M.M. (2010). Human Nonverbal Courtship Behavior—A
Brief Historical Review. *The Journal of Sex Research, 47*(2),
171-180.

Men often don't approach an inviting woman
Guéguen, N., Fischer-Lokou, J., Lefebvre, L., & Lamy, L. (2008).
Women's Eye Contact and Men's Later Interest: Two Field
Experiments. *Perceptual and Motor Skills, 106*(1), 63-66.

We overestimate how much sex everyone else is
having, perhaps due to entertainment consumption
American College Health Association. (2002) *National College
Health Assessment: Reference Group Report.* Baltimore,
MD: American College Health Association.

Chia, C. S., & Gunther, A. C. (2006). How media contribute
to misperceptions of social norms about sex. *Mass
Communication and Society, 9*(3), 301-320.

## Are We More Sexless?

Average number of sexual partners
Ueda, P., Mercer, C.H., Ghaznavi, C., & Herbenick, D. (2020).
Trends in frequency of sexual activity and number of sexual
partners among adults aged 18 to 44 years in the US,
2000-2018. *JAMA Network Open, 3.*

Zimmer-Gembeck, M., & Collins, W. (2008). Gender, mature appearance, alcohol use, and dating as correlates of sexual partner accumulation from ages 16-26 years. *Journal of Adolescent Health, 42*(6), 564-572.

## "Normal" Doesn't Mean Happy

Technological advances driven by social anxiety
Biddle, S. (2015, May 19). Silicon Valley Is a Big Fat Lie. GQ.

Comparing our insides to other people's outsides
Vorauer, J. D., & Ratner, R. K. (1996). Who's going to make the first move? Pluralistic ignorance as an impediment to relationship formation. *Journal of Social and Personal Relationships, 13*(4), 483–506.

## "If Dating Anxiety Is so Common, How Come I Feel so Alone?"

The relationship between social anxiety and shame
Swee, M. B., Hudson, C. C., & Heimberg, R. G. (2021). Examining the relationship between shame and social anxiety disorder: A systematic review. *Clinical Psychology Review*, 90, 102088.

What prevents two single people from dating
Vorauer, J. D., & Ratner, R. K. (1996). Who's going to make the first move? Pluralistic ignorance as an impediment to relationship formation. *Journal of Social and Personal Relationships, 13*(4), 483–506.

## Dating Anxiety: The Wound Even Time Won't Heal

The fundamental human need to belong and benefit of relationships
Baumeister, R. F., & Leary, M. R. (1995). The need to belong: Desire for interpersonal attachments as a fundamental human motivation. *Psychological Bulletin, 117*(3), 497–529.

Dush, C.K., & Amato, P. (2005). Consequences of relationship status and quality for subjective well-being. *Journal of Social and Personal Relationships, 22*(5), 607-627.

Men are lonelier than women, and may
suffer more unrequited love

Koenig, L.J., & Abrams, R.F. Adolescent loneliness and
adjustment: A focus on gender differences. In: Rotenberg
K.J.,& Hymel S., editors. *Loneliness in Childhood and
Adolescence*. Cambridge, England: Cambridge University
Press; 1999.

Hill, C.A., Blakemore, J.E., & Drumm, P. (1997). Mutual and
unrequited love in adolescence and young adulthood.
*Personal Relationships, 4*(1), 15-23.

Health impact of loneliness

Holt-Lunstad, J., Smith, T. B., & Layton, J. B. (2010). Social
relationships and mortality risk: A meta-analytic review.
*PLoS medicine, 7*(7), e1000316.

Cacioppo, J., Hawkley, L., Norman, G., & Berntson, G. (2011).
Social isolation. *Annals of the New York Academy of
Sciences, 1231*(1), 17-22.

Hawkley, L.C., Thisted, R.A., Masi, C.M., & Cacioppo, J.T. (2010).
Loneliness predicts increased blood pressure: 5-year
cross-lagged analyses in middle-aged and older adults.
*Psychology and Aging, 25*(1), 132-41.

Dush, C.K., & Amato, P. (2005). Consequences of relationship
status and quality for subjective well-being. *Journal of
Social and Personal Relationships, 22*(5), 607-627.

## Social Anxiety Is Chronic and Unremitting

Social impact on established relationships

Porter, E., & Chambless, D. (2014). Shying away from a good
thing: Social anxiety in romantic relationships. *Journal of
Clinical Psychology, 70*(6), 546-61.

People with social anxiety delay treatment
or don't seek it at all

Chartier-Otis, M., Perreault, M., & Bélanger, C. (2010).
Determinants of barriers to treatment for anxiety disorders.
*The Psychiatric Quarterly, 81*(2), 127–138.

Wang, P., Berglund, P.A., Olfson, M., Pincus, H.A., Wells, K.B., & Kessler, R.C. (2005). Failure and delay in initial treatment contact after first onset of mental disorders in the National Comorbidity Survey Replication. *Archives of General Psychiatry, 62*(6), 603-13.

Erwin, B.A., Turk, C.L., Heimberg, R.G., Fresco, D.M., & Hantula, D.A. (2004). The Internet: Home to a severe population of individuals with social anxiety disorder? *Journal of Anxiety Disorders, 18*(5), 629-46.

Schneier, F., Johnson, J., Hornig, C.D., Liebowitz, M., & Weissman, M. (1992). Social phobia. Comorbidity and morbidity in an epidemiologic sample. *Archives of General Psychiatry, 49*(4), 282-8.

Social anxiety is chronic and unremitting
Davidson, J. R., Hughes, D. L., George, L. K., & Blazer, D. G. (1993). The epidemiology of social phobia: Findings from the Duke Epidemiological Catchment Area Study. *Psychological Medicine, 23*(3), 709–718.

Stein, D. J., Lim, C. C., Roest, A. M., De Jonge, P., Aguilar-Gaxiola, S., Al-Hamzawi, A., ... & Scott, K. M. (2017). The cross-national epidemiology of social anxiety disorder: Data from the World Mental Health Survey Initiative. *BMC medicine, 15*(1), 1-21.

Reich, J., Goldenberg, I., Goisman, R., Vasile, R., & Keller, M. (1994). A prospective, follow-along study of the course of social phobia: II. Testing for basic predictors of course. *Journal of Nervous and Mental Disease, 182*(5), 297–301.

Russell, G., & Shaw, S. (2009). A study to investigate the prevalence of social anxiety in a sample of higher education students in the United Kingdom. *Journal of Mental Health, 18*(3), 198–206.

Avoidance, high performance demands,
and self-focused attention increases anxiety
Abramowitz, J. S., Deacon, B. J., & Whiteside, S. P. H. (2019). *Exposure therapy for anxiety: Principles and practice* (2nd ed.). The Guilford Press.

Hofmann, S. G., & Otto, M. W. (2008). Cognitive-behavior therapy for social anxiety disorder: Evidence-based and disorder-specific treatment techniques. Routledge/Taylor & Francis Group.

Meta-analysis showing intervention reduces
dating anxiety and increase dating behavior
Allen, M., Bourhis, J., Emmers-Sommer, T.M., & Sahlstein, E. (1998). Reducing dating anxiety: A metaanalysis. *Communication Reports, 11*(1), 49-55.

CHAPTER 2

. . .

# Why Am I Afraid of People I Want to Date?

I needed to find out why evolution had screwed me.

My quest started after a trip with my friend Ben. We were spending a week in Seville, the beautiful and ancient city in the south of Spain. We spent our days walking down winding, medieval streets, going to museums, ducking into random courtyards, and doing touristy things like watching flamenco dancers and drinking delicious wines. We stayed in a classic little stucco Spanish hotel adorned with bright colors and ornate tiles.

One morning, as I left the hotel, I noticed a woman talking to the clerk at check-in. She was animated, brightly-dressed, clearly Spanish, and I found myself so intimidated I could barely look at her. She didn't notice me, and I didn't say hello to her, but I saw her several other times over the next few days.

After our week of fun in Seville, Ben and I were preparing for the next leg of our trip, a short stay in a little place called Cordoba, famous for its baths. We headed to the central train station. We'd originally planned to spend some of our time in Seville traveling by Vespa and camping in a picturesque part of the area, so I'd bought a tent before we'd arrived. But things hadn't worked out. I didn't want to just throw away a perfectly good tent, but there was no way I was going to lug it around Spain for weeks on end. So as we waited in the train station, I decided to see if I could give it away to a fellow traveler.

As I turned a corner, I came face-to-face with the Spanish woman from the hotel. She looked at me warmly.

I blurted out, "Hi! Would you like a tent?"

She smiled at me, and my brain stopped functioning. Once we locked eyes, I could no longer summon any more words, English, Spanish, or otherwise.

My anxiety took over and shut me down. I was excruciatingly aware of how awkward I was being, but for the life of me I couldn't imagine how to interact with her. Ben was only a few steps behind, so he walked up and helped out. He wasn't interested in her, so he was very comfortable and talked freely. The two of them started chatting as I stood there dumbly.

She didn't need a tent, Ben discovered, but she was really friendly, and we somehow ended up at a coffee shop in the train station, discussing all the cool things we could do in our upcoming travels. I was painfully aware that her attention was locked on Ben, and I was nothing but a blank-faced simpleton in their presence. I wanted to speak, but I had nothing to say, and I couldn't process anything but my own anxiety. It was awful for me.

Eventually, we parted ways. But that wasn't the end. Weeks later, after I'd left Spain, Ben stayed behind and met up with her in her hometown. He sent me pictures of the two of them in front of landmarks they visited together.

About 20 minutes into the train ride out of Seville, I noticed my brain slide back into place, as though it had exited through the back of my skull while that woman was around. As I played the experience back in my mind, suddenly all the things I could have said popped in. I don't mean cool things I could've said, like the comebacks we generate long after someone is rude to us. I mean I was now aware of what I naturally would have said under normal conditions—things like basic questions, responses, easy jokes, and comments. Things that I inexplicably didn't have access to.

The frustration was overwhelming. *How come when it mattered the most, I was at my worst instead of my best?*

I returned from that trip determined to figure it out. *Isn't evolution all about trying to pass my genes on? Shouldn't it set me up to be at my best around women I'm into?* It just didn't make sense to me, so I threw myself into evolutionary research of psychology and social anxiety to figure it out—most importantly the amazing work of Paul Gilbert, Ph.D. What I discovered has completely reshaped my understanding of dating anxiety.

> You didn't choose to have dating anxiety, so there's no point criticizing yourself for having it. Instead, try being kind to yourself.

## Dating Anxiety Saved Your Ancestors

Here's what I learned: your dating anxiety is trying

to help you. It's a built-in self-protection system with a series of mechanisms intended to save you from social injuries.

Evolution provides us with adaptations that were helpful to our ancestors. Strange as it may sound, dating anxiety is one of those beneficial adaptations. We're born with a threat system that's designed to protect us from danger. How could this have been useful?

Let's say your ancestor was faced with a saber-toothed tiger. That ancestor's threat system got triggered, meaning they released adrenaline for strength, alertness, and physical energy. They switched to short, powerful breaths to flood their system with oxygen. Their pupils dilated to improve focus and eyesight. Their attention narrowed to scan and observe for threats. Because these threat responses were evolutionarily hardwired into our ancestors' nervous systems, they had a higher chance of survival.

But what if you encounter a magnetic person instead of a saber-toothed tiger?

More often than not, you'll have the same response. When our emotional brains sense something dangerous might happen, even if it's not physically dangerous, the same threat system kicks in to help us. As you can imagine, it's hard to be cool, witty, relaxed, friendly, creative, and smooth when you're faced with a dangerous tiger—well, it's the same when you're faced with someone you find really attractive.

## The Involuntary Submission Response

If you put a small animal in a cage with a larger animal, the small one is in danger. If they were to meet in the open, a small animal could escape, but in a cage there's nowhere to go. So what does this small animal do to find safety? It communicates through body language that it's not a threat, it's not going to challenge, and it accepts the other's superiority. In short, it communicates submission.

Here's what animal submission often looks like:

- Avoiding eye contact
- Inhibiting behavior, freezing, standing still
- Turning the body away
- Making itself as small as possible
- Not making sounds
- Not making claims on resources
- Backing down quickly
- Fear grinning

- Shaking
- Hiding and escaping if possible

Does that description sound familiar? It should—we do the same thing when we're socially anxious around powerful people. In animals, the goal of these behaviors is to make themselves small and quiet so they don't get injured or killed. In ourselves, the goal of these behaviors is very similar: we don't want to be socially attacked.

This cluster of behaviors is called "involuntary submission." As the name suggests, it's an automatic communication of lower social status. Weaker animals act this way to prevent being attacked, and it works. Most within-group conflicts in the animal world are solved through body language rather than physical fights, which helps preserve the strength of the group as a whole—the dominant one doesn't have to risk injury to establish their place atop the hierarchy, and the submissive one doesn't have to suffer physical defeat to accept a lower position.

*What if you thought about your dating anxiety as an automatic protection system—an involuntary submission response—that kicks in against your will?*

When I started looking at my own dating anxiety in this way, it made a ton of sense. I didn't *want* to convey fear, weakness, and submission, but I couldn't help it. Now I knew why.

**OTHER EXAMPLES OF THREAT RESPONSES**

- Being hyper-vigilant and scanning the room for potential threats.

- Focusing on yourself and trying to perform so well that people don't criticize you.

- Not expressing your true thoughts or opinions for fear of upsetting or turning off others.

- Not showing how much you like somebody for fear of rejection.

## Why am I Afraid of People I Want to Date?

Okay, so it makes sense that you would show submission around a large aggressive person in order to prevent getting beaten up. But why exactly does our brain perceive danger in talking to an appealing stranger, especially if they're open and smiling warmly at you?

*What are we so afraid of?*

First, you must understand the difference between actual rational dangers, and what our emotional brain has been primed to fear. These less rational fears are deeper, weirder, younger, hazier, and less grounded in reality. And most often we don't really know what we're afraid of until we dig.

I had one patient who gave me an honest depiction of his anxiety.

I asked, "What exactly do you imagine going wrong if you initiate a conversation with a woman?"

He thought for a moment before saying, "I imagine saying *Hi* to her, then she makes a disgusted face and kicks me in the balls. Or maybe she calls the police."

I've known multiple patients who were afraid that a hidden boyfriend, lurking just out of view, would swoop in to protect his girlfriend with physical violence at the smallest attempt at conversation.

But the vast majority of my patients fear someone's personal power. They fear their ability to inflict not a physical injury but a *social* injury—an anxious fantasy often complete with an audience pointing and laughing, the loss of social status, and a damaged reputation. Many people fear the look of disgust from that person, a social signal they believe will clearly communicate how far down the social hierarchy they really fall.

On a deeper level, all these fears convey a basic concern: by showing romantic interest in someone, you're doing something wrong.

One college student I worked with compulsively avoided looking at women he found attractive at his school. When I asked him why, he told me he believed his gaze was so unwanted that it was offensive. "Looking at women feels like rape," he said.

At the core of dating anxiety is a deep, evolutionarily-understandable belief that you will be punished for attempting to get something you don't deserve, and you'll be punished for breaking a social rule. There's an understanding that it's wrong (and even offensive) to show interest in somebody who's too far above you in the social hierarchy. Thus our brains activate a protective, defensive response.

Displaying romantic interest isn't as dangerous as our anxiety would have us believe. So why does it *feel* dangerous?

## Our Evolutionary Need for Acceptance

Why do we even care so much what other people think of us? After all, let's say I get harshly rejected in a bar in front of a bunch of people. Worst case scenario, I just go to the bar next door.

Well, it wasn't always this way. Our brains haven't changed for at least 35,000 years, and the best info we have suggests that humans used to live in groups of around 148 people. What those people thought of us was very important.

Humans have always been a very social species. Our default thought process—what we think about when nothing else is going on—is focused on our relationships. It also makes up the bulk of our conversations. That's because our ability to work as a group is one of our greatest strengths. A single human alone in the wilderness was (and is) likely to die fairly quickly. In our evolutionary past, if you didn't follow the rules of the group, there was a reasonable chance you'd be ostracized and die.

In present day, being kicked out of a social group isn't deadly—it's annoying. But in the past, you needed others for survival, and there were likely no other groups hanging around nearby eager for you to join. Even falling down the status hierarchy meant less access to resources, food, and mates (essentially, a harder and less rewarding life).

In short, we've evolved to find social injury almost as threatening as physical injury because it's so important to our success and survival. In fact, social and physical pain are processed the same way in your brain—you can even take ibuprofen to dull the pain of social rejection. We have innate psychological processes keeping us aware of our standing in the group, warning us against bad social behavior or breaking rules, as well as forming how we feel, think, and respond to social situations. This system may be especially sensitive to our perceived mating value.

Our levels of stress hormones are highest when we perform badly in front of an audience because our self-esteem is strongly influenced by how much we believe others value us. We are built to care about belonging, and we're built to be very wary of potential disapproval from the social group.

Acceptance by the group is very important to us, and the safest way to maintain group membership is to keep your head down, follow the rules, be humble, and not risk conflicts or challenging others for more resources.

From that context, it's strange to think there's anyone who *doesn't* experience dating anxiety.

## The Social Anxiety Equation

Now that you know where this dating anxiety comes from and why it exists at all, let's consider how this translates into the modern world.

You enter a social situation and your emotional brain senses potential danger. It fears that:

1. Your perceived flaws will be revealed
2. People will notice your flaws
3. They will also consider them flaws
4. They will be judgmental of your flaws
5. This will lead to harsh rejection
6. The rejection will be unbearable

This chain of beliefs is built up like dominos, and they knock each other down in a flash. Once the equation has been triggered, your threat system is automatically activated, and all of your self-protection mechanisms kick in to save you: self-focused attention, high performance standards, worry and rumination, involuntary submission, your urge to escape, and all the physiological symptoms (like shaking, increased heart rate, shallow breathing). This is the full-blown experience of dating anxiety, and it feels very different than the Warm Social World of spending time with close people who already like and accept us.

Here's the real kicker: despite its evolutionary origins, our automatic threat system response doesn't actually solve our problems in the modern world. Instead, it actively prevents us from achieving our deeply desired social goals: love and romantic connections.

Here's the truth: we're not going to be physically attacked for being friendly to people we find attractive. Someone turning us down doesn't lead to group humiliation, ostracism, and death. It's not likely to affect our social status at all. Our world doesn't consist of 148 people like our ancestors—we can find connections all across the globe.

But what if you're the exception? I had one patient raise the following point when I told him about our outdated threat system.

"Maybe the threat system knows what it's doing, and we should only pursue people who don't make us anxious? What if this is evolution's way of telling us where we stand in the social hierarchy?"

He went on to say that evolution is a manifestation of survival of the fittest, therefore his lack of dating success meant he should be removed from the gene pool.

I couldn't fully articulate it at the time, but I vehemently disagreed. We can't confuse evolutionary systems with clear realistic assessments of situations we encounter in our daily lives. Our emotional brain doesn't understand how the modern world works. Our threat system isn't realistic and accurate. In fact, it's not even meant to be accurate.

Our threat system is built on a "better safe than sorry" approach. It would prefer you to overestimate risk and avoid something rather than take a risk in the hopes of building a better life. The classic example is walking through the woods and seeing a long skinny brown object on the path in front of you. Your threat system is inclined to assume it's a snake and engage self-protection mechanisms (such as adrenaline rush, urge to escape, and hypervigilance), rather than run the risk of assuming it's a stick. Generations of people have survived to pass on their genetic material by assuming that risks are much higher than they truly are.

As a result, our threat system is uniformly and predictably inaccurate, and our anxiety exaggerates dangers. Engaging in these protective and submissive defenses when they're not needed can turn off others around you, and can keep you from making connections you could have otherwise made. This means that dating anxiety can and will kick in when there is little to no risk. Trust me: you can still feel dating anxiety even when you're around someone you know likes you.

## Don't Run From Your Anxiety

Remember this: just because you're anxious doesn't mean you're in danger.

Sure, dating anxiety kicks in when you're at risk of rejection, but it also kicks in when you have a really good shot at success. Therefore, it could actually make sense to have a rule where you only attempt to connect with people who trigger your dating anxiety. They're the ones you're actually interested in!

That's what I suggested when I treated a university student with dating anxiety. He was quite charismatic and had no trouble making friends. So what made him seek treatment? He'd experienced several successful relationships, but he only pursued people who made it very obvious they were interested in him. That way he didn't have to take any risks. These wound up being "relationships of convenience" since he didn't go after people he *really* liked. He only tried with people who really liked him.

A big part of his treatment was to become aware of his anxiety around rejection. Then, rather than interpreting his anxiety as a reason to avoid a potential partner, he chose to interpret it as something different: evidence that he was interacting with someone worth risking a connection with. To his surprise, he began dating the first person he pursued, and left treatment shortly afterward.

If we're built to run away from social risks, how come people don't all have the same level of dating anxiety? It comes down to a few individual factors: the particular combination of genes you inherited from your parents, how reactive your nervous system was from birth, the attachment experiences you had with parents or caregivers, beliefs from early childhood on your value, attractiveness, risks of rejection, and your social experiences throughout life. All of these factors have been shown to have some impact on your social anxiety levels in adulthood.

For the most part, the factors that gave you dating anxiety are out of your control, such as your genetics and attachment experiences with your parents. They're cards that make up a hand you've been dealt. Luckily, you get to choose how you play that hand going forward. You didn't choose this. It's not your fault. It's not fair. But you're the one left to figure it out. As we move forward, we'll identify the defense mechanisms you've developed to protect yourself from potential rejection and social injury, and slowly pry the clutching fingers of your threat system off of you, one by one.

## Our Biggest Gift from Evolution

Fortunately, evolution also gave us a tool to work with our miscalibrated dating anxiety: a really powerful neocortex. In other words, we've got a very big brain.

As humans, we're not completely at the mercy of instincts and emotional processing systems that are unconscious and operate against our will.

We also have executive functioning and the ability to be self-reflective. We're able to step back, observe our emotions and behaviors, organize and make sense of them, and override our instincts with deliberate choices. This is what allows us to engage in the specific therapeutic interventions we'll continue discussing in this book.

In fact, you've already been doing this since you started reading. Don't believe me? Ask yourself:

*Are you starting to understand your experience of anxiety a little differently?*

*Have you been able to step back from what you go through and observe your life?*

*Have you noticed that your observations have influenced the emotions you feel, perhaps edging you towards hope or a greater sense of calm?*

I trust you answered "yes" to at least one of those questions. If so, we'll continue to use our evolutionary gift of a high-functioning brain to intervene on your behalf. We'll then start to subdue and balance your automatic emotional systems. You'll talk to this part of your brain in a language that it understands: real world experience.

I know that's what I wanted to do after I got home from Spain. When I saw those pictures of my friend Ben with the Spanish woman we met in the train station, I was despondent. But I knew if I could just discover why my defense system had kicked on when I first met her, I could also figure out how to turn it off. In other words, if I could discover *why* I'd been so tongue-tied around her, I knew there'd be hope.

But hope isn't always easy. Hold on tight, because we're about to encounter information that might contrast sharply with your deeply held emotional beliefs. Beliefs you've developed to reinforce your threat protection system. It might be scary, but don't worry. As we test out just how threatening the social world really is, you'll see how easy it is to turn the tables on anxiety and use evolution in your favor.

CHAPTER 2 REFERENCES

# Why Am I Afraid of People
# I Want to Date?

## Dating Anxiety Saved Your Ancestors

Here are some core Paul Gilbert papers on the
evolutionary understanding of social anxiety

Gilbert, P. (2001). Evolution and social anxiety: The role of
    attraction, social competition, and social hierarchies.
    *Psychiatric Clinics of North America, 24*(4), 723–751.

Trower, P., & Gilbert, P. (1989). New theoretical conceptions
    of social anxiety and social phobia. *Clinical Psychology
    Review, 9*(1), 19–35.

Gilbert, P., & Trower, P. (1990). The evolution and manifestation
    of social anxiety. In W. R. Crozier (Ed.), Shyness and
    embarrassment: Perspectives from social psychology (pp.
    144–177). Cambridge University Press.

Gilbert, P. (2000). The relationship of shame, social anxiety
    and depression: The role of the evaluation of social rank.
    *Clinical Psychology & Psychotherapy, 7*(3), 174-189.

## The Involuntary Submission Response

Articles supporting the concept of involuntary submission

Gilbert, P. (2000). Varieties of submissive behavior as forms of
    social defense: Their evolution and role in depression. In
    L. Sloman & P. Gilbert (Eds.), *Subordination and defeat: An
    evolutionary approach to mood disorders and their therapy*
    (pp. 3–45). Lawrence Erlbaum Associates Publishers.

Gilbert, P. (2001). Evolution and social anxiety: The role of
    attraction, social competition, and social hierarchies.
    *Psychiatric Clinics of North America, 24*(4), 723–751.

Social anxiety (and shame) linked to submissive behaviors
Walters, K., & Inderbitzen, H. (1998). Social anxiety and peer relations among adolescents: Testing a psychobiological model. *Journal of Anxiety Disorders*, 12(3), 183-98.

Weeks, J., Heimberg, R., & Heuer, R. (2011). Exploring the role of behavioral submissiveness in social anxiety. *Journal of Social and Clinical Psychology, 30*(3), 217-249.

Zimmerman, J.A., Morrison, A., & Heimberg, R. (2015). Social anxiety, submissiveness, and shame in men and women: A moderated mediation analysis. *The British Journal of Clinical Psychology, 54*(1), 1-15.

## Our Evolutionary Need for Acceptance

People lived in groups of 148
Dunbar, R.I. (1992). Neocortex size as a constraint on group size in primates. *Journal of Human Evolution, 22*(6), 469-493.

Thinking (and talking) about relationships
is our default activity
Iacoboni, M., Lieberman, M., Knowlton, B., Molnar-Szakacs, I., Moritz, M., Throop, C., & Fiske, A. (2004). Watching social interactions produces dorsomedial prefrontal and medial parietal BOLD fMRI signal increases compared to a resting baseline. *NeuroImage, 21*(3), 1167-1173.

Dunbar, R.I., Marriott, A., & Duncan, N.D. (1997). Human conversational behavior. Human Nature, 8(3), 231-246.

Being kicked out of the group was a death sentence
Williams, K. D., Forgas, J. P., & von Hippel, W. (Eds.). (2005). The social outcast: Ostracism, social exclusion, rejection, and bullying. Psychology Press.

For animals the risk is physical injury,
for humans the risk is social injury
Gilbert, P. (2000). The relationship of shame, social anxiety and depression: The role of the evaluation of social rank. *Clinical Psychology & Psychotherapy, 7*(3), 174-189.

People fear loss of social status
Zhang, L., Liu, S., Li, Y., & Ruan, L.-J. (2015). Heterosexual
    rejection and mate choice: A sociometer perspective.
    *Frontiers in Psychology*, 6, Article 1846.

Social pain is processed as physical pain
Eisenberger, N. (2012). The neural bases of social pain:
    Evidence for shared representations with physical pain.
    *Psychosomatic Medicine, 74*(2), 126–135.

Dewall, C. N., Macdonald, G., Webster, G. D., Masten, C.
    L., Baumeister, R. F., Powell, C., Combs, D., Schurtz, D.
    R., Stillman, T. F., Tice, D. M., & Eisenberger, N. I. (2010).
    Acetaminophen reduces social pain: Behavioral and neural
    evidence. *Psychological Science, 21*(7), 931–937.

## The Social Anxiety Equation

Secondary social anxiety - anxiety about
anxiety, or shame about anxiety
Zimmerman, J.A., Morrison, A., & Heimberg, R. (2015). Social
    anxiety, submissiveness, and shame in men and women:
    A moderated mediation analysis. *The British Journal of
    Clinical Psychology, 54*(1), 1-15.

## Don't Run From Your Anxiety

What causes social anxiety?
Stravynski, A. (2014). Social phobia: An interpersonal approach.
    Cambridge University Press.

CHAPTER 3

. . .

# Take Off Your Armor

No one cares about you...at least not in public. One of my favorite researchers, Thomas Gilovich (with his colleagues), has done a bunch of wonderful studies supporting this assertion. His studies found that in most public settings people don't notice our embarrassing clothes, awkward behaviors, what we said or did, or whether we were even there in the first place!

Everyone is so wrapped up in their own lives that they barely notice ours.

I had to test the hypothesis myself. I firmly believe that each of us has tons of assumptions about our social environment (like what is acceptable and what isn't), but we never test the validity of those assumptions.

So I enlisted the help of my friend Ben for an experiment: we'd go out into a crowded bar and do something embarrassing to see if anyone noticed. We tried to figure out the most awkward and humiliating thing that could happen in public. What was our deepest fear?

Ben said, "What if a girl yelled at us for having syphilis?"

"I'm not scared of people thinking I have a venereal disease," I said. "I'm scared of being obviously, publicly rejected and having my embarrassing vulnerabilities revealed." I thought for a moment then said, "What if we got a girl to loudly reject us and tell us we have a small penis?"

"Small penis? I'm in."

We enlisted the help of his roommate, Liz, to act as the woman rejecting him at the bar. Before we went out to enact the experiment, he gave me his prediction for the evening:

"Liz will reject me, everyone in the bar will notice, they'll stop what they're doing and laugh, decide that I'm a loser, tell their friends, and make me completely undatable to everyone in the bar and their entire social networks."

He then swore at me for convincing him to do this and we made our way to the first venue.

We entered a hipster bar in Brooklyn with low lights, tons of people, and music playing in the background. It was terrifying and perfect. The experiment had begun. Ben walked up to Liz at the bar and gamely tried to talk to her.

She turned around and said in the loudest, harshest tone possible, "Get away from me, small penis!"

It was clearly audible over the music and chatter. It was so embarrassing I had to turn away. When I peeked back, I realized something: nothing had happened. Nobody stopped their conversation, nobody laughed or pointed, or even looked in their direction.

When Ben, Liz and I reconvened, we thought maybe the competing noise inside had drowned out the rejection, so we'd try again in the beer garden out back. Ben approached Liz, she screamed at him to get away with his small penis, and we waited for the responses.

Even in the quieter environment, nobody seemed to notice or care. Then a girl came up to Ben. He braced for an insult or admonishment, but she just asked him for a cigarette.

We went to another bar to try again. Then another. And another. Despite our initial fear, Ben received zero blowback or negative reaction of any kind. In fact, after Liz loudly rejected him at one bar, he easily talked to the group of girls nearest him, and one even gave him her phone number.

As the dutiful researcher I am, at every bar I asked people whether they'd seen that one guy with the small penis get humiliated. None of them had any idea what I was talking about. It was now clear that the research was correct: people don't care about us as much as we think, even when we get loudly rejected.

Now, a word of clarification: if we'd conducted these experiments at a library or college classroom, the outcome might have been different. Context does matter. But in the context of a busy bar, nobody gave a damn. You're in the background of other people's lives, and that should be a huge relief. You don't have to worry about how you hold your drink or what your hands are doing. You can let go of control, take risks, and feel confident that even if someone loudly rejects you, nobody cares!

## The Hypervigilant Crowd

One common element in dating anxiety—wonderfully articulated by social anxiety researcher David Moscovitch, Ph.D.—is the myth of the hypervigilant, hypercritical, gossiping audience. Until proven otherwise, we assume people are mean and judgmental. And we also assume that we are the center of everyone's attention, such that they'll catch our every flaw and misstep in an effort to tear us apart. Unfortunately, these assumptions keep our threat system activated because we feel like we're always in a dangerous social environment. We feel we must raise our performance standards to satisfy this tough audience, and we need to be highly self-conscious to monitor our behavior and estimate how we come across.

But what if all of our assumptions are wrong? What if we're essentially invisible and free to be ourselves in the social world? That would certainly make things easier.

Viewing the world through the lens of dating anxiety causes us to put up myriad social protections. Over time, those protections become armor. And it's uncomfortable, stiff, and hard to connect with people when you're in a suit of armor.

In this chapter, I'll dismantle this myth of the hypervigilant, hypercritical, gossiping audience. You'll learn that you're an extra in the background of any social setting, that people are largely empathetic and nice, and that there is very little risk of you being recognized and having your social reputation ruined.

Let's take off your armor and start connecting.

## The Charisma of Being Uncool

In my twenties, I fought mightily to achieve the gargantuan task of appearing as cool as possible at all times. I went out a lot, but never felt like I was coming across well enough or making a good enough impression. I listened to bad advice that suggested people were constantly judging everything I did and assessing my social value. Therefore, I had to micromanage every impression I made.

For example, one blog said you can't ever be seen standing alone not talking to somebody because then you look awkward and friendless, and that will drop your social value. So I always had someone around me. As soon as I was left alone, I got really anxious and would desperately look around for someone to talk to, whether I felt like talking or not. Somewhere else I'd read that you should always be moving with purpose and looking confident. Why? Who the hell knows. Maybe because anxiety makes you hesitate and second-guess yourself, so nobody with anxiety could move with purpose. After reading this garbage, I found myself walking around trying to appear purposeful when in fact I had nothing to do at all, and talking to people even though I had nothing to say.

Hell, I even used to struggle figuring out the coolest way to hold a drink. I read somewhere that holding your drink up high on your chest makes you look weak and anxious. Cool, confident people on the other hand hold their drinks down low. My friend questioned me at the bar about this one time.

"Why are you holding your drink way down towards your crotch? It looks weird."

I explained the theory, and he gave me an incredulous look.

"Do you really think people notice that?"

"Yes, they're watching everything I do down to the most minute detail!" I remember it sounding a little wrong even as I said it.

"Really? You're so important that people actually give a shit about where you hold your drink?"

As it turns out, the answer is a fat, resounding no.

## The Spotlight Effect

I get it. You feel like you're the center of attention in social situations. It sure seems like people pay attention when you're walking around, and surely they'll notice if you do something awkward or uncool. While you're far from alone in thinking this, you're also wrong. This is a cognitive bias known as "the spotlight effect," whereby you feel like there's a spotlight on you as you're walking around, so everybody pays attention to you.

There's a series of famous psychological studies about the spotlight effect. They compare how observable we think we are with how much people actually notice us. One study, orchestrated by Thomas Gilovich, involved putting college students in Barry Manilow t-shirts and testing how much this was noticed by other students during a brief social interaction. Barry Manilow has the ignominy of being picked because he was the uncoolest figure they could identify at the time: a puffy-haired crooner from the seventies, famous for managing to make Brazilian beach life seem lame with his hit "Copa Cabana." The study found that participants vastly overestimated how much others were paying attention to their embarrassing clothing. The t-shirt wearers estimated that about 50 percent of the students would notice their embarrassing attire. But when Gilovich asked the students, only 25 percent of them reported noticing the t-shirts. While you might personally be super aware of your clothes, it's likely that other people are not. We are far less

noticeable than we think. And it's not just our clothing—people often don't even notice we exist.

> Ever had the experience where someone tells you
> about an event, not remembering that you were there?
> If our friends don't even notice whether we showed
> up, imagine how little random people think about us.

So why is there this gap between how noticeable
we feel, and how much people actually notice us?

On one hand, because we are so noticeable to
ourselves, we just assume that others notice our
moods and actions too. But in reality, to most people,
we're just not that bloody interesting! Sure, our closest friends might notice our ups and downs more
than others. But seriously, out in an average social
situation—like at a bar or a cafe or walking around—
you're probably boring. There's a high threshold
required to get people's attention because, like you,
everyone is focused on themselves. Especially as a
stranger, nearly every thought they have is more
interesting to them than you are: how they're
being perceived, their own internal monologue,
how they're feeling, what's happening in their conversations, what their friend really meant by their
comment a few hours ago, and so on. You'd have to
try really hard to be attention-grabbing in that set-

ting (holding your drink too high isn't going to cut it) because you have to compete for attention with other things people *already* care about.

The average person couldn't give a shit about us—and thank god for that.

## Attention Is Finite

I know what you're thinking: "That's all good and well when you're in a bar with a bunch of stimulation. But what if I'm somewhere quiet? Then people will surely notice me."

Not necessarily. Attention is a finite resource, meaning if a person points their attention in one direction, they have less of it available to point elsewhere. In other words, people cannot pay close attention to everything or everyone simultaneously.

---

**GORILLAS IN OUR MIDST**

People will miss very obvious sights and sounds if they're told to focus their attention on something specific.

The most famous example is a study that asked people to watch a video of several people playing basketball. The study participants were then tasked with counting the number of passes each team made. The students were largely accurate in their count, but because their finite attention was focused on that task, the majority of observers missed something that should have

---

been obvious: a man in a gorilla suit walked into the middle of the game, beat his chest, and sauntered off. The effect is so striking that when I used to show the video in undergraduate classes, people thought I was showing them a different video with the gorilla.

This principle applies even in quiet environments. One of my patients, who is a librarian, told me of several occasions when she was unable to get people's attention away from what they were doing even in the very quiet environment of the library. In one case, she was literally yelling "Fire!" as the students around her remained absorbed in their computers. Another time, a sewer pipe burst, spewing disgusting sludge across the floor of the library. After evacuation alerts over the loudspeaker had failed to elicit any reaction, she had to individually tap students on the shoulder so they could avoid the river of grossness running across the floor.

I commonly go to coffee shops with patients to test their socially anxious assumptions. One patient in particular felt like she was being scrutinized at all times. We stood in line, allowing time to see if anyone noticed her. Nobody did. People were uniformly absorbed in their phones, their laptops, and their conversations.

So we escalated. We said things really loud, we dropped change, and fumbled her sunglasses.

Again we looked to see who was paying attention. The occasional person would glance, but only for a second before pulling back to what they were doing. One time, another patient brought a massive dictionary, at least six inches thick, and dropped it on the floor of a quiet coffee shop. It was very loud, but nobody gave us more than a fleeting glance. By the end of these treatments, each patient had largely overcome the assumption that anyone cared about them in public.

I imagine some people could see this invisibility as depressing. My patients often feel it as a liberation. You'll never be more socially free than when you realize nobody is paying attention to you. You are part of the background of everyone else's lives, which means you can be yourself, and do whatever you want without worrying that people are constantly monitoring you.

And even if people *do* notice you, strangers are a lot kinder than we give them credit for.

## Underestimating the Empathy of Strangers

When we experience dating anxiety, we assume the people who notice us are critical until proven otherwise. Now, plenty of people were mean in middle school and high school, but life isn't a teen movie—it's been documented that we underestimate the empathy of others. We tend to grow up and become kinder. In fact, I've had several patients who realized that much of their social anxiety came from believing that the social rules of middle school still applied in the real world. They don't. People are not rewarded with high status for being jerks to everybody when they grow up—it's just the opposite. Yes, there are some jerks in the adult world, but based on my own experiences and numerous experiments with my clients, I'd guess only 5% of people are true jerks.

People are raised to be nice. For the most part, they feel bad when they treat other people negatively. And there's even research that gives us a clue to what encourages empathetic treatment of others.

It's something scientists have called the mirror neuron system. Its existence became known through a series of primate studies showing that an observer's brain will light up like a mirror to the brain of whoever they're observing. In other words, when we watch somebody go through an emotional experience, we experience a little of that emotion ourselves. Ever notice that when somebody embarrasses themselves, you feel some embarrassment yourself? Far from criticism, judgment and the desire to attack, you tend to feel empathy and shared concern for the sufferer. These responses are an example of the mirrored neurological response.

My favorite example is the "Boom goes the dynamite" video. It was a viral video where a young man named Brian Collins floundered while trying to do the sports for a college news channel. He was just filling in, and it was his first time on camera. He appeared anxious and was clearly struggling to read the teleprompter. At one point, he dropped the phrase "boom goes the dynamite" while describing a three-pointer in a basketball game, and the phrase took off.

Watching the video is four minutes of agony. You'd imagine it represents public embarrassment, the display of flaws, and social failure. But that's not how we respond to it. We don't attack him. Instead, we feel for him. Whenever I showed this video in my classes, I didn't watch the screen—I watched the audience. All faces were twisted in empathetic embarrassment, as the students' experience mirrored the broadcaster's.

Although we haven't been through his exact experience, who hasn't stumbled while speaking in public? We all have, so we respond with empathy, not hate. Research shows that when people can imagine themselves in someone else's shoes, they tend to be far less critical. That's how potential romantic partners and the general public respond if you embarrass yourself in public: "We feel for you, man!" We have empathy if we've been through an experience like that as well. We know how awkward and scary it is to ask someone out and get shot down.

One study about embarrassment showed that everybody does embarrassing things all the time. On average, we do something we're embarrassed about once a week. Examples include: tripping on the sidewalk, spilling a drink, wearing stained clothes without realizing, forgetting someone's name, and having a bad hair day.

And do you feel like you embarrass yourself more often than everybody else? Guess what: that's what all the participants in the research study said. We underestimate how often others do embarrassing things because, unlike that sportscaster, the world never finds out about it. We also underestimate how empathetic others will be towards us when we embarrass ourselves. We don't realize how often others have the same struggles we do.

Imagine how much easier it would be to take social risks, reveal who you authentically are, and go after what you want if you knew that people are generally kind and empathetic?

## The Blessing of Bad Memory

It's hard to get over the fear of interacting with potential romantic partners in public. When I first started this research, I feared that I'd screw up socially and forever be known as "that guy who got humiliated one time." In my mind, I'd always be recognized as somebody with low social status. How likely is that? After tons of research, I discovered the answer: not very likely.

People are terrible at remembering a face they see just one time.

This research emerged out of an understanding that eyewitness testimony was usually inaccurate, and memories are easily twisted or changed over time. Many studies were conducted with bank tellers testing whether they were able to identify robbers. These studies found that even trained professionals under ideal conditions forgot the faces of people they'd seen almost *immediately*.

Researchers identified five factors required to remember and retrieve a once-seen face (keep this in mind any time you're worried someone will remember you for an imperfect social performance):

1. Your face must be seen for at least a full minute. Anything less than that will not be seared into people's memory.
2. The environment must have clear lighting and good visibility.
3. Attention needs to be focused on your face and nowhere else.
4. The observer must have consumed no alcohol, even low levels of blood alcohol disrupt the encoding of new memories.
5. Your appearance cannot have changed in any way since the event. Any change in appearance very quickly disrupts the ability to recognize a once-seen face.

### WHO ARE YOU AGAIN?

Therefore, since it takes a long while before we understand a face enough to recognize it when it changes, simple changes in hairstyle, eyewear, facial hair, and even lighting can make you unrecognizable to strangers. And even close friends...

As a teenager, I once failed to recognize my best friend after he cut his long hair into a buzzcut. It took him standing in front of me and saying his name before I caught on.

Now let's apply this information to our fears around public rejection. First, consider what social environments are generally like. Many social environments, such as bars and clubs, are specifically designed to ease anxiety, since anxiety is an expected human experience in these scenarios. On top of the constant distractions, the lighting is kept low, and alcohol is prevalent. As you can see, the same things we do to lower social anxiety also reduce people's ability to remember your face.

In basic terms, you're good. Go ahead and take some pro-social risks and embarrass yourself all you want to. Even if someone is watching you (which they aren't), no one will remember who you are anyway.

## What's the Worst-Case Scenario?

Still not convinced you're not the center of a judging crowd's attention? Let's give you a useful last line of defense. Let's ignore all the evidence and research we've just gone over and assume that everything you fear comes true: you attempt to start a conversation with a person you like and you get shot down (or you do something embarrassing or some flaw gets revealed) and, against all odds, people are momentarily more focused on you than on their own lives.

On top of all that, they not only see you get rejected, but they actually *care* that it happened. Not only *that*, but because everyone other than you has experienced nothing but anxiety-free social acceptance, they judge you harshly for being rejected. And, miraculously, somehow the lighting is good enough that everyone can see your face and remember you.

Now your life is ruined. Word will spread throughout your community. Your status will drop so low that no one you like would ever date you—right?

Nope, not even in the worst scenario. No one will gossip about you because you're just not important enough. The research says that in order to make your public humiliation worthy of other people's gossip, people have to know you personally or you have to be famous. Why? Because gossip is only compelling if the person being discussed matters to the listener. As Gary Fine—a gossip researcher and professor of sociology—put it, "We gossip about people we care about. We don't bother talking about people who don't matter to us."

Think about the biggest celebrity stories of the year. A pair of famous singers get married. An actor buys a new home. A news anchor gets fired. Now imagine instead of celebrities these stories involved some random people who lived in your friend's neighborhood. These fascinating dramas suddenly become boring non-stories, all because you don't care about the people involved.

The point is: even in a worst-case scenario, you are way safer than you realize in social settings. So why not drop that armor?

## It's Time to Drop the Armor

Contrary to how you might feel about the social world, you're actually okay out there. You're not a celebrity. Therefore, people aren't scrutinizing your every move. You don't have to be on guard. As such, we've poked some holes in the fearful assumptions that drive social anxiety. As a reminder, these beliefs are that:

1. Your perceived flaws will be revealed
2. People will notice your flaws
3. They will also consider them flaws
4. They will be judgmental of your flaws
5. This will lead to harsh rejection
6. The rejection will be unbearable

In reality, the science we've discussed suggests people likely won't notice our flaws and screw-ups.

And if they do, most people have embarrassed themselves in public, too. Everyone has flaws. Almost everyone is more empathetic and less rejecting than we think. Even if they are judging you, it's not the end of the world because people forget and move on.

I tell you all this so you feel emboldened to take risks in the service of connecting with people. Because what I'm about to suggest will require courage: I want you to drop the armor. Stop doing all those little things you do to protect yourself from judgment, social injury, failure, and status loss. I want you to drop the self-protection and move towards connection. Think about it: nobody can connect with someone in a suit of armor. How can you even hug or kiss a potential partner when you're covered by clunky metal? It's impossible. So let's start by identifying a few common pieces of armor you might be carrying around:

- Focusing attention on yourself to make sure you don't screw up
- Scanning for potential threats
- Avoiding or escaping anxiety-provoking social situations or interactions
- Trying to make a great impression

- Trying to hide your anxiety and perceived flaws
- Not showing your romantic interest
- Never risking rejection

You wear that armor because some part of you is trying to protect you, and it believes you need this armor to be safe. Sear this into your mind: your anxiety is not the problem. *Your real problem is this self-protective behavior.* Each of these behaviors actually increases your anxiety, while decreasing your chance of connection.

## Two Principles for Treatment Going Forward

### Principle 1: We need to face social situations even though they make us uncomfortable.

Probably the most basic principle in anxiety treatment is that you have to move towards the thing that triggers your fear. Part of the reason anxiety gets worse over time is that what works in the short term backfires in the long term. If you avoid something out of fear, your fear will increase over time.

On the flipside, if we repeatedly face something we're afraid of, without protections, our anxieties will decrease. Even more importantly, repeatedly throwing yourself into social situations is necessary to practice everything I'm teaching you. Plus, how will you make connections if you don't venture into the social world more? The assumption from here on out is that you'll move towards situations you find uncomfortable. You don't have to do the super scary stuff (yet), but you must start moving forward into the Warm Social World rather than hanging back in the World of Threat.

### Principle 2: We can't assume that our current beliefs about the social world are correct.

We all have cognitive biases, like the myth of the hypervigilant, hypercritical, gossiping audience. Our anxiety only heightens these biases. So how did we develop our current social beliefs?

We learn to see the world in a certain way when we're young, and those beliefs stick around because we never actually challenge them. Scientists, on the other hand, learn to assume their hypotheses are incorrect, and set up experiments specifically to challenge their preconceived notions. We can do the same with our social beliefs. We don't have to assume our negative beliefs about the social world are accurate. We can instead consider them as hypotheses, and test their validity with behavioral experiments (the term we use in therapy for putting these beliefs to the test in our social lives). Merely reading new information is not enough to change your life, even though it's fun and the information here is awesome. Experience is more important—that's the only way our emotional brains truly learn.

## One Step Further

Based on these two principles, I want to pose a different hypothesis: you are safer than you feel in public. In fact, I'd take it a step further. That's not a hypothesis—that's *the truth*. If you believe that, you might have just enough courage to do the hard work I'm asking of you. In order to get where you want to go, you must drop your defensive armor.

Letting loose and having fun requires a lot of courage. But imagine how easy your life would be if you didn't feel the need to protect yourself socially. Dropping your protection and moving towards something you're afraid of is scary. And yet, this is how we grow.

Whenever I feel like all eyes are on me in a social setting, I remember how free I felt that night in Brooklyn when I was experimenting with my friends. We could have yelled out the nuclear launch codes in every bar we went to, and nobody would have given a damn. Everyone is so concerned with their own lives that they don't even think about you. So go ahead and drop the armor.

Now let's push that idea a step further.

I don't even want you to focus on you! I want you to be that person who's genuinely curious about the people around you. Because here's the deal: if you can drop your socially protective armor, you're in great shape. But if you combine that with shifting the spotlight to people around you, you'll become less anxious and more engaging.

Here's how...

# CHAPTER 3 REFERENCES

## Take Off Your Armor

People aren't as aware of us as we think

Gilovich, T., Medvec, V. H., & Savitsky, K. (2000). The Spotlight Effect in social judgment: An egocentric bias in estimates of the salience of one's own actions and appearance. *Journal of Personality and Social Psychology, 78*(2), 211–222.

## The Hypervigilant Crowd

The myth of the hypervigilent, hypercitical audience

Moscovitch, D. A. (2009). What is the core fear in social phobia? A new model to facilitate individualized case conceptualization and treatment. *Cognitive and Behavioral Practice, 16*(2), 123–134.

## The Spotlight Effect

The Spotlight Effect

Gilovich, T., & Savitsky, K. (1999). The Spotlight Effect and the illusion of transparency. *Current Directions in Psychological Science, 8*(6), 165–168.

People won't notice your Barry Manilow T-shirt

Gilovich, T., Medvec, V. H., & Savitsky, K. (2000). The Spotlight Effect in social judgment: An egocentric bias in estimates of the salience of one's own actions and appearance. *Journal of Personality and Social Psychology, 78*(2), 211–222.

## Attention Is Finite

Gorillas in our midst

Simons, D. J., & Chabris, C. F. (1999). Gorillas in our midst: Sustained inattentional blindness for dynamic events. *Perception*, 28(9), 1059–1074.

## Underestimating the Empathy of Strangers

Mirror neurons review

Jeon, H., & Lee, S. H. (2018). From neurons to social beings: Short review of the mirror neuron system research and its socio-psychological and psychiatric implications. *Clinical Psychopharmacology and Neuroscience: The Official Scientific Journal of the Korean College of Neuropsychopharmacology, 16*(1), 18–31.

People are less critical than we think

Moon, A., Gan, M., & Critcher, C.R. (2019). The overblown implications effect. *Journal of Personality and Social Psychology, 118*(4), 720–742.

Savitsky, K., Epley, N., & Gilovich, T. (2001). Do others judge us as harshly as we think? Overestimating the impact of our failures, shortcomings, and mishaps. *Journal of Personality and Social Psychology, 81*(1), 44–56.

We have empathy if we have been
through similar experiences

Regan, D. T., & Totten, J. (1975). Empathy and attribution: Turning observers into actors. *Journal of Personality and Social Psychology, 32*(5), 850–856.

People embarrass themselves regularly

Epley, N., Savitsky, K., & Gilovich, T. (2002). Empathy neglect: Reconciling the spotlight effect and the correspondence bias. *Journal of Personality and Social Psychology, 83*(2), 300–312.

## The Once Seen Face Fallacy (or The Blessing of Bad Memory)

We are bad at remembering the once-seen face

Deffenbacher, K.A., Bornstein, B.H., McGorty, E.K., & Penrod, S.D. (2008). Forgetting the once-seen face: Estimating the strength of an eyewitness's memory representation. *Journal of Experimental Psychology: Applied, 14*(2), 139-150.

Valentine, T., Pickering, A., & Darling, S. (2003). Characteristics of eyewitness identification that predict the outcome of real lineups. *Applied Cognitive Psychology, 17*(8), 969–993.

Kong, S.G., Heo, J., Roui-Abidi, B., Paik, J., & Abidi, M.A. (2005). Recent advances in visual and infrared face recognition—a review. *Computer Vision and Image Understanding, 97*(1), 103-135.

Tollestrup, P., Turtle, J., & Yuille, J. (1994). Actual victims and witnesses to robbery and fraud: An archival analysis. In D. Ross, J. Read, & M. Toglia (Eds.), *Adult Eyewitness Testimony: Current Trends and Developments* (pp. 144-160). Cambridge: Cambridge University Press.

White, A. M., (2003). What happened? Alcohol, memory blackouts, and the brain. *Alcohol Research and Health, 27*(2), 186-96.

Westrick, E.R., Shapiro, A.P., Nathan, P.E., & Brick, J., (1988). Dietary tryptophan reverses alcohol-induced impairment of facial recognition but not verbal recall. *Alcoholism: Clinical and Experimental Research, 12*(4), 531-534.

## Who Are You Again?

Simple changes can make you hard to recognize

Posamentier, M.T., & Abdi, H. (2004). Processing faces and facial expressions. *Neuropsychology Review, 13*(3), 113-143.

## What's the Worst-Case Scenario?

We don't gossip about random people we don't know

Westen, R., (1996). The real slant on gossip. *Psychology Today, 29*, 41-46.

CHAPTER 4

. . .

# Shift the Spotlight

Have you ever been so immersed in a movie that you completely lost yourself? Have you identified with a main character so deeply that you sat in a dark theatre and forgot you're a person?

You're so absorbed in what's happening on the screen that you're not thinking about yourself at all. You're not processing whether your hands are in the right place, how you might look to other people, or if what you're doing is appropriate. Instead, you're fully engaged in what's happening in front of you. Then the movie ends, and you remember who you are, where you are, and it's almost like you wake up to yourself again. While watching that movie, your attention was fully external. And I'm willing to bet that while you were externally focused—despite being in a room full of strangers—you weren't feeling any dating anxiety (unless, of course, you were on a first date—in which case you may have never lost yourself in the movie in the first place).

In this chapter, we'll once again narrow our scope from the social world at-large to the dating world specifically. As such, I'll encourage you to stop focusing your attention on yourself in potential dating situations. I'll ask you to stop analyzing yourself because self-focused attention is one of the quickest ways to escalate your anxiety. Even worse, it disconnects you from people and can lead to awkward social behavior. Instead, you'll consciously focus your attention away from yourself and towards other people. I'll coach you to notice what's happening in your world, which entails seeing the best in others, and being genuinely curious about other people. I think you'll find this makes dating a lot easier and more comfortable.

## Can You Reverse-Engineer Confidence?

Although the research on this was well-established at the time, I stumbled into the importance of externalizing attention while studying something else entirely. I'd been contemplating how my social life changed based on how I felt at the time. I noticed after I'd had a good social interaction (one in which someone flirted with me, for example, or they gave me their number) the world felt different. Everywhere I looked, I saw people who were warm, friendly, happy to socialize, and possibly interested in me. I saw potential everywhere. In this Warm Social World, it was so much easier to start conversations and meet new people.

On the other hand, if it had been a while since I got any acceptance, or I was having a bad acne day, the world appeared cold and uninviting. In the World of Threat, I had to fight myself just to look at people. I *expected* rejection.

"How much easier would dating be if I was in that positive mental state all the time?" I thought. I wondered if I could reverse-engineer social confidence and give it to myself whenever I wanted. I went out that night to test it.

I met up with some friends in a pool hall, a popular place usually full of college students. Even before I got there my threat system kicked in. As I entered, my attention focused almost entirely on myself, just like always. I quickly scanned the room and saw an intimidating group of beautiful women and guys who were bigger and more attractive than me. Looking at them, I felt my attention shift toward my shortcomings. As I imagined how I must look to these people, I was abundantly aware of my flaws—I saw myself as short, skinny, acne-prone, nervous, awkward, and inferior to the people around me. I went into my head, imagining all the things that could go wrong if I talked to this threatening group of people and how I might try to prevent it all (stand taller, look tough, go get a drink, hide my anxiety). I felt the threat chemicals pumping through my body, triggering anxiety symptoms and compelling me to collapse into involuntary submission.

None of this was new—it was my usual anxious experience. But that night, testing out something new, I recognized that I didn't feel this way at all times.

I was able to step back and observe my experience of anxiety without buying into it. I reminded myself that sometimes I felt confident and open. With that thought in mind, I forced myself to look at everything around me through those eyes. I thought about the way I processed the world when I was feeling good, and I tried to purposely do that in the pool hall that night.

I deliberately looked for the good in people around the room. Instead of considering those around me as potential enemies who could socially injure me, I assessed them as potential allies.

"What would make that person a good friend? What are their strengths?"

To do this, I had to actually *look* at them. Not a quick glance before turning away, but a true external assessment. I looked at the intimidating women, and I noticed that they were smiling, laughing, and having fun with the people around them. I looked at the athletic guys too, and saw they were mostly warm and open. As I looked closer, I saw that a few seemed stiff and uncomfortable, perhaps even anxious. Immediately, I noticed my mood lift, and I felt warmer toward everyone in the room. As I moved around the pool hall with this feeling, I noticed something that changed my life:

*As I radiated warmth and openness, people reflected that warmth and openness back to me.*

There's a common adage I first heard from Eckhart Tolle that I think holds true: "Whatever we think the world is withholding from us, we are withholding from the world." That was no more true for me than in that moment. I walked past everybody, and rather than switching to my self-focused obsession with my perceived flaws, I externalized my attention and observed and appreciated the good in people.

Later in the night, I realized the intimidating group I'd noticed before was right behind me, hanging around the Big Buck Hunter arcade game. As I turned to look at them, I locked eyes with a young woman. I smiled, she smiled back at me, and we started talking.

What happened next? I'll tell you. But first, before you can understand the full weight of what happened in that pool hall, I need to teach you some fundamentals about awareness and attention.

## The Attentional Flashlight

Think of your attention like a flashlight. Wherever you shine this flashlight, that area gets brighter, and everything else darkens. As we move through the world, there are overwhelming amounts of stimuli available to us. There's far too much happening—in the world, in our thoughts and memories, in our body sensations, in our emotions—for us to pay attention to everything at once. As a result, evolution has provided us with a mechanism that allows us to focus on only the most important stimuli, while simultaneously allowing everything else to fade into the background. For example, if you're at a loud hipster bar in Brooklyn having a conversation with your friends, you won't likely notice a random girl harshly rejecting some guy on the other side of the room. Or while you're reading this, you're likely not aware of the feeling of your body in the chair, or the feeling of the socks on your feet, the scent in the air, background traffic noise, or the air conditioner—until I pointed them out. We have the ability to aim our flashlight of attention in any direction we choose, and that is one of our most underused and counterintuitive resources in overcoming dating anxiety.

Most people aren't aware of where their attentional flashlight is pointed. Ask yourself: what percentage of the time is your attention external, engaged with the world, and processing what's happening around you? And what percentage of the time is your attention inside your head, focused on your own thoughts, memories, and worries about the future? This is fundamentally important to know. A big reason why mindfulness and being present-focused have recently entered the zeitgeist is that they all require you to focus your flashlight of attention on what's happening externally—outside of your thoughts, and often outside of your body—

which only occurs in the present. A focus on the past or future is necessarily an *internal* focus.

And when we start to focus internally, it's a short ride to the land of negative ideas, self-criticism, and anxiety. Research shows that the more we worry about the future, the more anxious we get, and the more we ruminate about the past, the more depressed we feel. In fact, one study found that the more time you spend in your head in general, the worse you feel.

## Pre-Event Worry in Dating Anxiety

If you tend to worry in the lead up to a social event, what percentage of the things you imagine going wrong actually occur? How many of the solutions you come up with do you actually use? Did you really need to figure out your talking points in advance? How bad would it be if there was a pause in conversation?

Many of us suffer through a strong experience of pre-event worry, also called anticipatory anxiety, in which you worry about social situations in the lead up to them. It's particularly difficult because the anxiety can last for weeks if the event is scheduled far enough in the future.

We tend to imagine the upcoming social event, creatively picturing myriad things that might go badly for us. This is followed by attempts to problem-solve these potential disasters, imagining how we might prevent them, or (less commonly) how we might respond if they happened. Unfortunately, as soon as we think of an answer to one problem, another takes its place. And then another. And then we go back and worry about that first one again. "What was my comeback if someone makes fun of my Barry Manilow shirt? And what if that line doesn't work?"

This is the pattern of pre-event worry, and it's a strong driver of social anxiety. Considered from the framework of the flashlight of attention, it's clear to see why. You're dedicating a lot of time to focusing on social failure and things going wrong, and research has found that the more we imagine a possible future, the more likely it seems.

It's hard, because worry feels like it should be helpful, but the evidence doesn't back this up. Most often, all that pre-event worry has no impact on the actual outcome, except that it makes you *much* more anxious and less confident going in.

Pre-event worry is such a powerful factor that changing this one thing alone can make a big impact on improving your dating anxiety.

## No Thinking Ahead

Dating anxiety strikes people at different parts of the process—some struggle most in advance, some in the moment, and some beat themselves up after. One of my long-term patients, Rafael, was good at being in the moment in social settings, and often forgot his fears once he was talking to someone. The problem was the lead-up. Though he knew he'd be fine once he got there, he couldn't help but stress for hours or even days leading up to a social event. He found his mind drifting back to worries about what might happen, and this wound him up and made him tense. It even interfered with other important aspects of his life, like work and sleep.

We used a fairly simple intervention: ban thinking about the dating event in advance. This was a stressful idea, because he felt things would go badly if he wasn't allowed to think about the date ahead of time. I challenged him to explain exactly why he needed to ponder it in advance. Rafael realized he was spending his time figuring out how to come across well, how he might stop people from judging him or seeing his flaws, what steps he had to take to make a connection, and by doing so he thought he could overcome potential problems. If he didn't do this, it felt like the social event would go badly.

"But I guess I'll try it your way," he said.

Shortly after that conversation, Rafael had a speed dating event. Leading up to the event, whenever he caught himself ruminating on it, he chose to not "think it through" and instead refocused his attention on work, friends, or whatever was happening in front of him.

Now, in the final hours leading up to an event, Rafael's anxiety usually ratcheted up. This time, to refocus his attention, he created a perfect solution: he scheduled a hangout with his friends in the bar next door immediately before the event started. That way he would be fully in the moment with his friends, feeling good and comfortable, and he'd just walk out of the bar and into the speed dating event with no time to worry.

When I talked to him next, he told me it was a great success. He was able to enter speed dating with openness and warmth, free of worry. As a result, his anticipatory anxiety was at a record low, and he had a great time. Although he didn't get any matches, he used this strategy successfully from then on.

## Post-Event Rumination or
## The Social Post-Mortem

When you leave a social event, are you fully in the moment, or do you go into your head, reliving what happened?

If you're like most people with dating anxiety, you're like an ESPN sports commentator after a social event. You're in your head, going over a play-by-play of the evening complete with stats and analysis. But rather than showing the highlights, you focus on your errors and misses. You might replay those again and again. Believe it or not, this behavior is another counter-productive, self-protective effort. We look back at the party, the date, or the hangout intending to identify what we did wrong so we can better protect ourselves from failure and rejection in the future.

But this "post-event rumination" is just as damaging as pre-event worry.

It's a seductive habit, but there's little benefit in going over your social performance afterward.

- Firstly, you have no videotape of your social events. Most research shows that whatever you remember is heavily skewed by your biases. In other words, you can't trust your memory.

- Secondly, you're likely to focus heavily on the negative aspects of what happened and ignore the positive and neutral interactions you had.

- Thirdly, on rare occasions, I've seen people make an insight by analyzing what happened during a date or interaction with a potential partner, then put that insight into action later. But more often, this process makes you feel bad and less likely to socialize next time. Probably for the same reason that having your dad yell at you about how poorly you played after a sporting event doesn't make you calm and happy for the next game. It lowers your confidence and increases your perceived performance standards. This is a recipe for anxiety.

**FOCUS ON THE MOMENT**

Some cutting-edge research—largely orchestrated by Adrian Wells, Ph.D., whose work strongly influenced this chapter—shows that you can reduce your social anxiety very significantly just by dropping the worry process before a social event, and the post-mortem assessment after the event. If you recognize when your attention has gone inside your head to worry or ruminate, choose to focus your attention back on the task at hand—there's always something of value that you're getting distracted away from in the moment. Focus on that instead.

## The Danger of Self-Focused Attention

Now consider where your attention goes when you're actually in the social environment and you're around people you find attractive, whether you're at a bar, on a date, or out in the park. Rather than focusing on what's happening around you, you're likely shining the flashlight of attention on yourself:

- "How do I look?"
- "What are people noticing about me?"
- "Do they see my flaws?"
- "Do I sound weird or boring?"
- "I hope I don't screw up again"
- "My heart is beating so fast."
- "I'm so anxious."

Again, this focus of attention is a clear self-protection behavior. You'd rather keep a diligently close eye on your social performance and catch a screw-up before someone else does. It doesn't work. Why?

## Self-Focused Attention Escalates Anxiety

When you focus attention on yourself, your anxiety goes up. And it goes up a lot.

If you have traits or anxiety symptoms you think could lead to rejection, you'll focus your attention on them. Let's use blushing as an example. If you blush, you'll likely focus a chunk of your attention on how hot your face feels and how you imagine you might look to others. In this case, your focus on your "flaw" leads you to feel worse about yourself and become more anxious. Secondly, your increased attention makes that symptom feel stronger or seem more obvious, which also increases your anxiety (the brightening effect of the attentional flashlight). In fact, there's evidence that our internal images of ourselves are negative exaggerations—like a carica-ture of yourself with a tomato-red face, in the case of blushing.

It's hard to feel relaxed and confident while you're focused on how pathetic you are. One study showed that you can create social anxiety in normally calm people simply by having them deliberately focus attention on themselves. Just imagining how you might look in the eyes of others will make you more anxious because you automatically look for flaws.

An easy way to conceptualize this connection between self-focused attention and anxiety is to think about where your attention goes when you're feeling calm and accepted in a social situation. When you're hanging out with close friends and family, where is your attention? When you're enjoying time with another person and having great conversation, how much of your attention is dedicated to noticing your behavior and physical sensations and what people might be thinking about you? Probably very little. You likely get lost in the activity, stop analyzing yourself, and feel good.

Imagine if you could have this feeling all the time. Even at the bar.

## Bar Games

When I discovered this research, I realized that I'd actually been using externally focused attention to cope with my anxiety since I was a young adult. This began with something my friends and I called "bar games."

I never felt comfortable going out to bars after I turned 21. I got really anxious, felt out of place, and had no idea what to do there. I decided the problem was this: for all other events, there was a clear activity involved—you went to a movie, you went bowling, you went to dinner, etc.—but when I went to a bar, there was nothing to do. You just stand around with a bunch of your friends waiting for something to happen. When there was nothing to do, I became self-conscious, uncomfortable, and very aware of myself. It was also boring. Out of necessity, I invented little games that lowered my discomfort by externalizing my attention or lowering my performance demands and gave me ways of having fun in these awkward environments. Over time, I started using these to target dating anxiety in general. Here are a few that are particularly fun or helpful, listed in order of difficulty (easiest first):

1. **The Best for My Friend Game—**This one is a really potent anxiety reducer. It works like this: instead of standing around thinking about how you are coming across, you walk around with a goal in mind: who do you think your friend would like best? It gives you something to do, engages your empathy and desire to help, and requires you to take attention off yourself. You don't

have to talk to the people you find (although you could). You just point out who you think your friend would like best and why, they do the same for you, and you see how right each of you is.

2. **The Say Hello Game**—The first person to say hello to five people wins. No need to say anything else after. This one is very simple, but incredibly powerful. The stakes are so low that it's easy to accomplish, but you get to meet tons of people and it puts you in a social mood.

3. **The Opening Line Game**—The point of this game is not to be offensive or vulgar, but to say the most boring opening line. The funny thing with this game is that the lower your bar of success, the better you actually do. I once won this game with my friends when I walked up to a girl who had injured her leg and was wheeling around on one of those temporary scooters. I said, "You have a hot wheelie." She laughed and we had a fun conversation.

4. **The Compliment Game**—This one isn't just about giving someone a compliment on their appearance. Your goal with this game is to compliment something on another person that you think most people wouldn't recognize. The beauty of this game is it gets you in the mindset of, "What's good about this person?" rather than looking for things to be scared of. I've made tons of friends and even met a girlfriend playing this game (although you shouldn't be playing this game thinking it will get you a date).

5. **The George Costanza Game**—There was an episode of "Seinfeld" where George Costanza did the opposite of everything he would normally do, and his life improved significantly. That's how you play this game. If you would normally make a joke, say something serious. If you'd normally order a Bud Light, order a Mojito. See what happens.

There are plenty of other bar games, but they center more on being goofy with your friends than anything else. The thing is, these bar games all help to lower your anxiety through externally-focused attention, reduced performance goals, mini-exposures, and behavioral experiments. There's no winning or losing—only having a good time.

## Self-Focused Attention Causes Weird Behavior

Patrick was a great engineering student, and he was tall, dark, and handsome, but he was struggling socially. He complained that when he was anxious, he couldn't think of what to say. In conversation, Patrick knew it was his turn to talk, but he'd stand mute, struggling while people looked at him expectantly. When we broke it down, it was really easy to spot the problem. Patrick was very concerned that he would come across as weird, and his defense was to constantly monitor himself to see whether he was appearing normal during conversations.

But in the process of avoiding awkwardness, Patrick came off as even weirder.

Patrick dedicated so much attention to appearing normal that he never really heard what people said to him. Then he didn't know how to respond because he hadn't actually processed what was happening in the conversation.

I had to teach him the lightbulb model of conversations. Here's how it works: in the best conversations, topics move around and new ideas arise organically. People with anxiety regularly complain of conversations that are stagnant, forced, or hard to continue and they want to plan out a better conversation. But it's not good to know where a conversation is going because it's meant to be a voyage of discovery, and we want to discover things as we go. As one person talks—which at its best is simply thinking out loud—the other person should be listening deeply to what's being said. If you let it, whatever the other person says will trigger a new thought or a lightbulb, so to speak.

> Imagine one of those old cartoons where a character gets an idea and a bright yellow lightbulb suddenly flicks on above their head. Ding!

In conversation, these lightbulbs might be memories that get triggered, opinions that get lit up, or new thoughts and ideas. Either way, in a lightbulb conversation, everything comes up as a natural reaction to what another person is saying. Then, when it's your time to speak, you want to express that new lightbulb idea. If you do, what you say will in turn light things up for your partner, and the cycle continues.

Patrick had no lightbulbs. He didn't listen closely enough for lightbulbs to flick on, and this had to change. So we came up with an intervention. His goal was to focus his attention on what the other person was saying, and then say something that was a direct response to what they said. Maybe he'd support what they said if that's how he felt, or he'd express an opinion about the topic, or his own related experience. This forced him to listen closely. He was required to accept the risk that he might appear abnormal or "weird," in his own words. We even experimented with a lightbulb game based on storytelling. I would tell Patrick a story, he'd think of a related story to tell, which would trigger me to tell another related story. We went back and forth as long as we could. This game was great for dropping his self-editing conversation filter.

When he returned to therapy after trying this, he was shocked. He'd had much better conversations, he was less anxious, and people responded more warmly to him. In particular, he noted that he always had something to say and he felt much more comfortable since he wasn't desperately trying to cultivate people's perception of him.

## THE SELF-OBSESSED NATURE OF ANXIETY

Self-focused attention can lead to awkward social behaviors. For example, being self-focused on any automatic normal behavior can make it feel unnatural. The most common example is becoming too aware of your hands and not knowing what to do with them. But you can become awkward about almost anything—how you walk, how you speak, your posture, how often you say "like" or "um," the words you choose, and so on. Any attempts to consciously control something that is typically unconscious can make you anxious and awkward. This doesn't happen when your attention is external and you allow yourself to be naturally imperfect.

Patrick had a hard time trusting that he could take the spotlight off himself and focus it on other people. He worried that his self-focus kept him safe and without it he'd act weird and people would reject him. Even though he came to realize this wasn't true, he is far from alone in his concern.

## People Like it When You Focus on Them

Most people love it when someone is curious about them. Externalized attention in the form of curiosity is a warm, wonderful social skill for connecting with people. It's especially powerful in dating. You stop thinking about yourself, and you put your energy into really listening to and understanding someone else. Oprah Winfrey said that humans, at their core, just want to be fully heard (and, I would add, accepted). In fact, most research shows that being curious is a huge driver of dating success.

To some extent, you already know the positive impact of curious attention because you've been on the receiving end of it. And you know how annoying it is for people to focus their attention away while talking to you (one example is someone looking over your shoulder as you talk, as if you aren't interesting enough). You've also had the subtle feeling of rejection when someone pulls out their phone to text during a conversation. In contrast are the people you've met who make you feel important, interesting, and that whatever you say really matters to them. The difference in those two feelings—the neglect of not being paid attention to and the joy of being heard and seen fully—is the social power of curious attention.

When discussing someone who is particularly charming you'll hear people say, "I felt like the only person in the room." That's because externalized attention is a powerful factor in flirtation. It makes people feel important. To hammer this point home, consider the words we use with attention: you *give* someone your attention or you *pay* attention to someone. It's so valuable that we talk about it with the same terms we use with money.

Something as simple as getting a little extra eye contact bumps up our physiological arousal. You could even argue that flirting is just a series of behaviors whereby you give more and more attention to another person. You smile more, ask more questions, spend more time with them, make more eye contact, touch more, etc.

If you can't focus your attention on someone else, you can't flirt. Get good at externally focusing your attention on others, and you won't just be less anxious, you'll also develop one of the most important dating skills.

## Notice the Positive Signals You're Already Getting

What if you could weaken your anxiety just by picking up the signs of acceptance that are already there?

Remember Steve, the guy from the start of the book who gave me six months to help him with his dating anxiety before he wanted to end his life? He came in one session looking particularly perplexed. I wondered out loud what had put him in this state. He'd been out on a terrible date the previous week, and we'd discussed it in-depth in our previous session. He said in the previous session that he'd liked her, but she wasn't into him. He felt he'd made such a bad impression that he never followed up with the woman.

Fast forward to our next session. He said, completely dumbfounded, "That girl from last week texted me. She asked me what she did wrong and how come I never asked her out again after such a great date."

Contrary to his assumption that she didn't like him, she did like him, and couldn't understand why he didn't ask her out on a second date. How could this be?

He was so focused on his internal experience of anxiety and self-criticism that he missed the inevitable signals of enjoyment and attraction she was sending. This is a surprisingly common problem, and it's an unexpected driver of social anxiety. If you get good social feedback, or signs of attraction, you don't want to miss them!

I asked him what he based his assessment of the date on. His response showed it was clearly *internal* information rather than externally observable evidence. He said he'd felt awkward, he'd been nervous, he'd screwed up, he didn't perform well enough, he was lame, annoying, uncool, weak, and any other negative adjective he could use to describe himself. Those of us with social anxiety tend to have a negatively skewed self-concept, so it's not good enough to base our assessments on internal information. Externalizing your attention will help you find more positive signals than you'll get from yourself. In other words, other people usually like you more than you like yourself.

### MISSING THE POSITIVE IN THE MOMENT

I got to see this process play out in great detail in a session with one client as I was writing this book. I arranged for Daniel, a patient of mine in his mid-thirties, to do a dating exposure interaction with an engaging young woman. The two got to know each other while I (somewhat awkwardly for everyone) observed. I was surprised at the end when he told me it went terribly. I had watched it all, and it went great!

I asked how he knew it went badly. Daniel said he just felt like he screwed up, didn't perform as well as he wanted to, and made a bad impression. I asked him for the evidence. Specifically, I asked him what he observed from the young woman he was interacting with. He acknowledged that when he thought about it, she had smiled, asked questions, and laughed at his jokes.

"So where is the direct, observable evidence that you did badly?"

He thought for a moment. "Maybe she was just being polite."

"Objection," I said, jokingly. "We don't accept mind-reading as evidence due to the fact it's impossible to do."

Daniel acquiesced that there was no observable evidence that he did badly.

"What about your other goals?" I asked. He was working on self-disclosing more and telling stories. "Did you meet them?"

"Yes, but I could have done better."

"Whether you could conceive of an ideal way to do it was not my question, that's just testing out your imagination. Did you meet your goals of opening up more and telling stories?"

"I guess I did, yeah."

I talked with the young woman afterward, too. She told me she had a very good time talking and he made a good impression.

If we had not intervened, Daniel would have left believing he screwed up and the woman disliked him—all based on his prioritization of internal evidence (imperfect performance, feeling uncomfortable, mindreading negative judgment, not getting a standing ovation, etc.).

It's also helpful to deliberately look for the positive in people's responses, since this helps overcome our innate negativity bias. We're inclined to interpret

neutral responses as negative, or to screen out pos-
itives and pay extra attention to the negatives. If we
get 9 pieces of positive feedback and 1 negative,
guess which we tend to think about the most?

## Ways to Improve Attentional Focus

### Curiosity Is the Answer

As I alluded to earlier, the easiest frame for improving attentional focus is this: be curious.

You can be curious on all kinds of levels: about
the world around you, the emotions of the person
talking to you, what someone is really trying to say,
and so on. Curiosity is also a core psychological intervention. It implies openness to new experience, and
a warm interest in the world. It makes others feel
good about themselves and it makes conversations
much easier. If you practice curiosity, you'll take a
step outside your negative thought processes, you'll
radiate warmth, you'll meet other people's needs to
be seen, and you'll reduce your own anxiety.

### Externalize Attention by Setting
### Appropriate Goals

One effective method of externalizing attention is to
set the right social goals. Some research has found
that socially anxious people tend not to have good,

clear, concrete social goals. Changing this alone can lower your anxiety.

Here are some examples of the *wrong* kinds of goals that I hear on a regular basis:

- Don't screw up.
- Make sure everyone likes me.
- Get someone to go out with me.
- Don't look anxious.
- Be impressive.

Can you see why these goals would be counter-productive? There are actually many things wrong with them, including setting high and unrealistic performance standards, and requiring mindreading to measure. Most importantly, these goals require self-focused attention. *In order to not screw up, I must monitor myself continuously. To make sure everybody likes me, I have to constantly measure whether I'm living up to idealized performance standards. To make sure I don't look anxious, I have to constantly imagine how I must look through the eyes of others.* Would you accept it if someone else watched you with that level of scrutiny? Then don't accept it of yourself.

Your social goals cannot be based on how you come across to others, or what they think about you. We don't even want goals that are based on how other people *respond* to us, since that's outside our control. Instead, goals should be certain behaviors that you will engage in that require (or at least encourage) you to be externalized, and that hopefully nurture curiosity.

Here are some of my favorite types of social goals:

- Identify a person who looks friendly, one who looks kind, and one who could use a smile.
- Introduce yourself to three people and find out what they're like.
- Self-disclose something new with people and see if they reciprocate.
- Find out something new about someone you've already met.
- Find out what makes a particular person interesting (everyone is interesting if you look hard enough).

## How to Build Your Attention Muscle

Plenty of us feel like we're just not very good at choosing where our attention goes. Even if we know we shouldn't focus internally, we can't always help it. Perhaps we have ADHD or we're easily distracted, or our anxiety just compels our attention towards potential threats. The good news is that attention is a psychological muscle that can be strengthened. You can build your attentional muscle by engaging in attention training. The best way I've come across to do this involves listening to multiple sounds simultaneously, but choosing to invest attention on only one particular sound at a time. This is exceptionally helpful because it trains you to focus on something despite many competing things trying to distract you (similar to what you might experience in a social setting).

Consider why this is useful: most of us operate on a belief that we can't focus on something unless there are no distractions. Our attention goes toward whatever stimulus is strongest and most attention-grabbing. That's why it's hard to read a book if someone is talking. We believe we must suppress all distractions first before we can focus on what we want.

However, suppression doesn't work when it comes to anxiety. We can't wait until we've suppressed anxiety before we focus our attention externally and engage with the world. Anxiety is too loud and insistent, and by engaging with it, we tend to escalate it. We can't solve an internal focus of attention by internally focusing our attention. Instead, we accept it's there, allow it to be loud and annoying, and choose to point the flashlight of attention externally anyway.

How does this play out in a dating situation? Well, first of all, you can't afford to wait until there are no distractions or until your anxiety has gone away before you start externalizing attention—it might not happen! Instead, practice allowing anxiety symptoms to exist in the background, but deliberately choose to focus externally (on whatever your social goal is). Attention training is a great way to do this.

The very influential psychologist Adrian Wells had fantastic recordings on his website to help you with attention training. Or you can create the training yourself by turning on the TV, music, listening to the traffic outside, and playing nature sounds on your computer. Then take turns shifting your attention to focus as much as possible on one particular sound, while accepting you cannot suppress the others and just leaving them alone.

I also encourage you to engage in regular meditation. This is broadly helpful in both the long term and short term, but it's particularly great for developing your attentional muscles. At its core, meditation is simply focusing on a boring stimulus (your breath or, even better, a mantra), from which the mind will inevitably wander. You then notice when your attention drifts into thought, and choose to refocus on the boring stimulus again. What is this, if not attention training? The research backs this up: regular meditators show improvements in attentional focus and emotional regulation. You don't need to practice for a long time—positive impacts were observable in as little as five days according to one study.

## Applying Practice to Real Life

In sports you practice regularly, then on game day you put the skills you practiced into action. The same thing goes for psychological growth. Practice attentional skills daily so you can rely on these in real-life situations.

You can even practice when you're getting groceries or walking to your car. Look at what's happening around you. Look at other people, look at all the colors, notice the sounds, and notice what's interesting. See what percentage of your attention you can focus externally. I do this with patients, and regularly see anxiety scores in the moment drop from 8 or 9 to 3 or 4 just by noticing their surroundings with intention. Adrian Wells refers to this as "situational attentional refocusing."

After a while, you want to get to a place where you can focus your curiosity on another person even while experiencing distracting thoughts, negative emotions, or uncomfortable body sensations. Sometimes, in my sessions, I have my patients engage in speeches or small talk while making these anxious distractors as intrusive as possible. For example, I have them do a bunch of push-ups or run around the building, and then come in and make small talk with a stranger while their body is full of typical anxiety symptoms like fast heart rate, shallow breathing, sweating, etc. At other times, I have patients make speeches while I turn on YouTube videos, make loud noises, or even have other people say anxiety-provoking things to them, like, "You're screwing up, everyone can tell you're anxious, you're mumbling, stop being weird." These techniques may sound harsh, but if you can get to the point where you focus on the task at hand despite powerful distractors, you'll be far less prone to social or dating anxiety.

Self-focused attention is meant to protect us, but it almost always backfires. Focusing your attention on how you come across increases your anxiety significantly. But if you forget about yourself and approach the world with curiosity, you might be surprised how much more comfortable you become.

What people think of as weird behavior is often nothing more than self-focused anxiety.

What people perceive as cool, smooth, and comfortable is often nothing more than other-focused curiosity.

## The Pool Shark, or Lack Thereof

Back to the pool hall from the beginning of the chapter. I was walking around the bar and pool hall, deliberately externalizing my attention and looking for the good in everyone I saw. As I looked for warmth, I easily found it—even when I saw a group of people I would've usually dismissed as shallow bullies.

Like I said before, I started talking to a girl. We immediately formed a natural and friendly connection. It was nothing like what my threat system had predicted, and something that very rarely occurred for me.

To be clear, there's no fairytale ending here. We didn't start dating or fall in love or get married. But that doesn't matter. We had a warm, friendly, positive interaction, and I felt great afterward. I enjoyed my time that night and I knew I was onto something. Not because I suddenly had a date or a girlfriend, but because I'd changed my goals, externalized my attention, and changed my experience. The world seemed warmer, I felt less anxious, and more open.

Once you drop your armor and externalize your attention, there's another step you can take. Remember at the beginning of the book when I said some of my advice might sound counterintuitive or odd? You're about to read one of the most counterintuitive chapters in the book—because I want you to make a *mediocre* impression.

# Shift the Spotlight

Most important papers on the role
of attention in social anxiety
Clark, D. M., & Wells, A. (1995). *A cognitive model of social phobia*. In R. G. Heimberg, M. R. Liebowitz, D. A. Hope, & F. R. Schneier (Eds.), *Social Phobia: Diagnosis, Assessment, and Treatment* (p. 69–93). The Guilford Press.

Nordahl, H. M., Vogel, P. A., Morken, G., Stiles, T. C., Sandvik, P., & Wells, A. (2016). Paroxetine, cognitive therapy or their combination in the treatment of social anxiety disorder with and without avoidant personality disorder: A randomized clinical trial. *Psychotherapy and Psychosomatics, 85*(6), 346-356.

Hofmann, S. G., & Otto, M. W. (2008). Chapter 3. Cognitive-behavior therapy for social anxiety disorder: Evidence-based and disorder-specific treatment techniques. Routledge/Taylor & Francis Group.

## The Attentional Flashlight

The more we worry the more anxious we feel
Wells, A. (2010). Metacognitive theory and therapy for worry and generalized anxiety disorder: Review and status. *Journal of Experimental Psychopathology, 1*(1),

Rumination can drive depression
Nolen-Hoeksema, S., Wisco, B. E., & Lyubomirsky, S. (2008). Rethinking rumination. *Perspectives on Psychological Science, 3*(5), 400-424.

More time in our heads makes us feel worse
Killingsworth, M.A., & Gilbert, D. (2010). A wandering mind is an unhappy mind. *Science, 330*, 932-932.

## Pre-Event Worry in Dating Anxiety

Worry drives negative expectations
Kelley, C.M., & Jacoby, L.L. (1998). Subjective reports and process dissociation: Fluency, knowing, and feeling. *Acta Psychologica, 98*(2-3), 127-140.

Just imagining rejection can lower self-esteem
Vandevelde, L., & Miyahara, M. (2005). Impact of group rejections from a physical activity on physical self-esteem among university students. *Social Psychology of Education, 8*(1), 65-81.

## Post-Event Rumination or The Social Post-Mortem

Post-event rumination
Hofmann, S. G. (2007). Cognitive factors that maintain social anxiety disorder: A comprehensive model and its treatment implications. *Cognitive Behaviour Therapy, 36*(4), 193-209.

Rumination can yield benefits if it focuses on correcting errors and goal attainment
Ciarocco, N.J., Vohs, K., & Baumeister, R. (2010). Some Good News About rumination: Task-focused thinking after failure facilitates performance improvement. *Journal of Social and Clinical Psychology, 29*(10), 1057-1073.

## Focus on the Moment

You can decrease social anxiety effectively with attentional changes and reducing worry/rumination
Nordahl, H., & Wells, A. (2018). Metacognitive therapy for social anxiety disorder: An A-B replication series across social anxiety subtypes. *Frontiers in Psychology, 9*, 540.

Vogel, P. A., Hagen, R., Hjemdal, O., Solem, S., Smeby, M. C. B., Strand, E. R., Fisher, P., Nordahl, H. M., & Wells, A. (2016). Metacognitive therapy applications in social anxiety disorder: An exploratory study of the individual and combined effects of the attention training technique and situational attentional refocusing. *Journal of Experimental Psychopathology*, 608–618.

## Self-Focused Attention Escalates Anxiety

Our internal self image is a negative caricature
and focusing on it increases social anxiety

Clark, D. M., & Wells, A. (1995). A cognitive model of social
phobia. In R. G. Heimberg, M. R. Liebowitz, D. A. Hope, & F.
R. Schneier (Eds.), *Social phobia: Diagnosis, Assessment,
and Treatment* (p. 69–93). The Guilford Press.

Spurr, J.M., & Stopa, L. (2003). The observer perspective:
Effects on social anxiety and performance. *Behaviour
Research and Therapy, 41*(9), 1009-28.

Anyone looks and feels more anxious
when made to self-focus

Woody, S. R., & Rodriguez, B. F. (2000). Self-focused attention
and social anxiety in social phobics and normal controls.
*Cognitive Therapy and Research, 24*(4), 473–488.

## People Like it When You Focus on Them

Curiosity helps with dating, self-focused attention hurts

Kashdan, T. B., & Roberts, J. E. (2006). Affective outcomes in
superficial and intimate interactions: Roles of social anxiety
and curiosity. *Journal of Research in Personality, 40*(2),
140–167.

Kashdan, T. B., & Roberts, J. E. (2004). Trait and state curiosity
in the genesis of intimacy: Differentiation from related
constructs. *Journal of Social and Clinical Psychology, 23*(6),
792-816.

Importance of externalized attention in flirtation

Egland, K. L., Spitzberg, B. H., & Zormeier, M. M. (1996).
Flirtation and conversational competence in cross-sex
platonic and romantic relationships. *Communication
Reports, 9*(2), 105-117.

## Notice the Positive Signals You're Already Getting

Missing positive signals due to self
focused on internal information

Cameron, J. J., Stinson, D. A., Gaetz, R., & Balchen, S. (2010). Acceptance is in the eye of the beholder: Self-esteem and motivated perceptions of acceptance from the opposite sex. *Journal of Personality and Social Psychology, 99*(3), 513–529.

Alden, L., & Mellings, T. (2004). Generalized social phobia and social judgments: The salience of self- and partner-information. *Journal of Anxiety Disorders, 18*(2), 143-57.

Hope, D. A., Sigler, K. D., Penn, D. L., & Meier, V. (1998). Social anxiety, recall of interpersonal information, and social impact on others. *Journal of Cognitive Psychotherapy, 12*(4), 303–322.

## Ways to Improve Attentional Focus

Benefits of improving goal setting in social anxiety

Hofmann, S. G., & Otto, M. W. (2018). Chapter 3. In *Cognitive behavioral therapy for social anxiety disorder: Evidence-based and disorder-specific treatment techniques,* Routledge.

Barber, K. C., Michaelis, M., & Moscovitch, D. A. (2021). Social anxiety and the generation of positivity during dyadic interaction: Curiosity and authenticity are the keys to success. *Behavior Therapy, 52*(6), 1418–1432.

Meditation improves attention and emotional regulation

Tang, Y., Ma, Y., Wang, J., Fan, Y., Feng, S., Lu, Q., Yu, Q., Sui, D., Rothbart, M. K., Fan, M., & Posner, M. I. (2007). Short-term meditation training improves attention and self-regulation. *Proceedings of the National Academy of Sciences, 104*(43), 17152-17156.

Norris, C. J., Creem, D., Hendler, R., & Kober, H. (2018). Corrigendum: Brief mindfulness meditation improves attention in novices: Evidence from ERPs and moderation by neuroticism. *Frontiers in Human Neuroscience, 12,* 342.

Verhaeghen, P. (2021). Mindfulness as attention training: Meta-analyses on the links between attention performance and mindfulness interventions, long-term meditation practice, and trait mindfulness. *Mindfulness, 12*(3), 564–581.

Attention training
https://mct-institute.co.uk

# CHAPTER 5

. . .

# Make a Mediocre Impression

"I just didn't know what to say. I couldn't think of anything good enough."

Mike, a patient in his late twenties, was sullen as he sat on my couch. He was smart, athletic, and driven. As you can guess, he didn't see himself that way. He had the problem of overly focusing on his failings. He'd come in to treat his long-term dating anxiety, which kept him out of any kind of romantic relationship for the bulk of his adult life. Like so many men with dating anxiety, he tended to clam up when he was around girls he liked. We were getting a little closer to figuring out why.

Mike was describing a recent interaction at work. Part of his job involved going to different companies' offices, and one office in particular had a receptionist he found very attractive. His most recent social goal was to interact with her a little more. He told me the last time he saw her, his mind went blank.

"What happened?" I said. "I have a hard time believing that your mind was producing no thoughts at that time. When people say they couldn't think of anything to say, they often mean they couldn't think of anything *good enough* to say."

He smiled sheepishly. "I was looking at her, and she was smiling at me and being friendly like she normally is, and I really wanted to connect with her. But I was thinking about how she's so attractive and kind, and how high her expectations must be for a guy, since she's the sort of person that *everybody* would like. So I tried to think of something that would be impressive enough for her. I needed to say something a cool, confident guy would say. But I couldn't come up with anything. So I said nothing and left."

"Wait, there are special things that only confident guys say, like secret words?" I was purposely being a little tongue-in-cheek. "What would be an example of that? What's something good enough that you could've said?"

He was quiet for a while. Finally, he said, "I don't know. I'm not a cool, confident guy so there's no way I can come up with what a cool, confident guy would say."

"So, by definition, nothing that you could think of to say would be good enough?"

"Yes."

"And therefore, by this rule, you can never speak around women you find attractive. Right?"

"Yes."

"That's going to be a bit of a problem."

The point of this chapter is that having high performance demands—trying to be impressive—works against us. The more you expect from yourself, the more anxious you'll get. Even worse, the higher those demands, the less likely you are to even try. The beauty of what I'm about to tell you is that you don't need to be impressive to connect with people. Time and time again, we'll see that the simplest, most fundamental social skills are the most effective at actually bonding with people.

If you stop trying to be impressive, you'll be less anxious, you'll interact more regularly, and you'll connect more effectively.

So let's make a mediocre first impression.

## Opening Lines Are Simple:
## Just Say Something

I used to struggle mightily starting conversations with people I found attractive. Starting conversations with everybody else was fairly easy, but with women I liked it was tough. I could never find the right thing to say, so, more often than not, I said nothing. I can't tell you the number of times I failed to talk to somebody because of this. I've exited countless other interactions too early for the same reason. Nowadays it's easy, since I know the real problem is not a lack of something "good enough" to say but rather the decision to self-protect and not say the things that naturally come to mind.

I was excited one summer when my research turned up a series of studies on the best opening lines in dating situations. "This is exactly what I need," I thought.

After extensive research I've discovered the most effective opening lines. Are you ready? Prepare to have your mind blown! Here they are. The best pickup lines in the world are:

"Hi, my name is _____."

"What's your name?"

"How are you?"

Yes, I was disappointed also. I thought the studies would turn up something witty. Something that made whoever said it appear cool, funny, intelligent, and sexy.

But no, it seems that basic, direct, or innocuous "lines," such as a simple introduction, appear to be the most likely to start a conversation. In fact, it seems that innocuous opening lines are even *better* than witty ones. The researchers in some of these studies actually sent people out into social settings to see which opening lines led to conversations lasting more than a few seconds. They tried other lines that were trying to be cute, witty, or bashful—essentially lines with more effort and less authenticity. (One of the examples was "Is that really your hair?") All the studies backed up the same principle:

*Starting a conversation with somebody is not a complicated performance piece.*

It's just basic social connection, so simple is best. Why might this be? Maybe because something like an introduction is expected, easy for another person to respond to, and it's substantially less cheesy than a witty line. Or, like one study suggested, it's because people using these simple opening lines seem "sociable and bright." Regardless of the reason why it works best, it's good news. An introduction or greeting is eminently more achievable and less anxiety provoking than trying to make someone like you from the outset.

## The Simplicity Principle

This simplicity principle—as I took to calling it—did fit with my experiences. My friend Ben is very friendly, and I always noticed how easy it was for him to start conversations. We would go to some social environment, and I'd be trying to think of something cool to say, and I'd turn around and find him already deep in conversation with somebody. He was certainly not impressive with his opening lines, if you can even call them that. He would literally say whatever popped into his mind, no matter how odd. He truly did not care. He just wanted to talk to people and he wasn't going to let a lack of having something impressive (or even relevant) to say stop him.

I remember him talking to a very tall woman in a cocktail bar in Boston, then he turned around to tell me, "She's from Serbia, so I just asked her about ethnic cleansing. She hates me!" Now, let me make one thing very clear: in that scenario, Ben did not make a socially acceptable introduction—I would never advocate talking about genocide as an initial topic of conversation. But it certainly demonstrates that you don't need to think of anything cool, witty, or impressive to say. Remember the lightbulb game I mentioned in the last chapter? The one where one person tells a story and the other person tells a story they think of in response? Ben lives life like he's playing that game on steroids. Whatever lightbulb idea hits him, he says it. Despite this sometimes-brash behavior, people love him. He's the most naturally socially successful person I know.

Over time, I noticed Ben had a common opening line that he said so often I started calling it "the sorry opener" in jest. Ben would bump into people all the time, or he'd stand in their way, or interrupt them while they were doing something, then he'd just say, "Sorry." The ice now broken, he followed immediately by saying whatever popped into his head. Things as noteworthy as, "This bathroom line is really long." Nothing impressive or witty, just "Sorry" and whatever he was thinking. But it's very important to note that he always said whatever he said with a big smile and a ton of warmth, because that's the secret: be unimpressive and have a big smile.

## The Boring Bar Game

Ben's "opening line" inspired The Boring Bar Game. I had a patient try the game as an experiment once. He was a naturally charismatic guy, but had previously been immersed in the Pickup Artist community online, which taught him that everybody was shallow and judgmental. Therefore, he felt he had to impress people with "displays of high value" at all times. As such, he had a terrible time getting over his avoidance and starting conversations. Even when he did interact with someone, he was so focused on being impressive that it stunted any connection he could make.

So we conducted a behavioral experiment. He was required to start conversations by being warm and boring. He had to say "Hi," smile, and ask the person about their day, comment on the weather, or some other topic he felt wasn't "good enough." Nothing weird, just boring and basic. Then he had to observe the person's response. He fully predicted negative reactions—dismissive facial expressions, rejections, and so on. But what he found was that people were uniformly nice, and some were very friendly. He got into a bunch of conversations and noticed that these went way better than his usual conversations. Simple social skills, even talking about the weather—literally the most banal topic in the world—were all he needed. And of course, he was significantly less anxious because he no longer had to perform.

> I often tell patients to consider their low anxiety, extroverted friends. How impressive are the things they say? Usually not very. And yet, how do others respond to them, and how are their social lives? In general, extroverts are not trying to be impressive, they're just saying whatever comes to mind, and it seems to go pretty well. You can observe the limits of what's acceptable from hanging around a low anxiety extrovert for a while.

One socially anxious patient told me that she went on vacation with her extroverted father, and he would talk to anybody within a 10-foot radius of them. He would ask them all the same three questions, and he'd have a variation of the same conversation again and again. She also reported that everyone appeared to have a great time doing it! She couldn't make sense of it—how was this going so well for him when he was so unimpressive? I explained that what they were enjoying was *the connection*, not the content. He enjoyed having a conversation and getting to know somebody. The conversation was just a vehicle for the connection to happen.

With that in mind, I ask you: what if the thing people respond to isn't the content of what we say, but the openness, warmth, and honesty that you convey in the process?

## Trying to Be Impressive Can Backfire

Trying to impress people is unnecessary. It makes us significantly more anxious, and substantially less likely to socially engage. It also makes you less likable and harder to connect with, because people aren't seeing the real you, they just see the front you put up. Think of your own experiences. I bet you don't like people better when they try to be impressive, or try to seem cool and valuable. If failing at coming across as impressive is bad, succeeding might be even worse: if someone is successful at coming across as more impressive than us, we often still don't like them. Rather than garnering admiration, you tend to garner envy at best, and derision at worst. Trust me, I know what happens when it goes badly. I tried this for a long time, and I got some pretty bad reactions. People connect so much more easily when you're authentic, unprotected, and focused on warmth and curiosity. Not to mention, sometimes the attempt to impress can backfire on you.

When I was young, clueless, and flailing around with no idea how to handle my dating anxiety, I worked in an independent video store in Boston's north end, and it was my dream job. I loved it because I talked to everyone who came in, I had time to do my homework, and I got to watch all the latest movies.

One day a girl I thought was really cute came in and we started talking. I felt like I wasn't good enough for her, so I thought I had to impress her. To that end, I told her, "Someone I used to date is on the current season of The Bachelor." It was such an odd thing to say, never mind the fact that it wasn't true. The girl on the show I was referring to was merely a girl who sat next to me in biology class when I was in college in California several years earlier. She was a girl I *wished* I'd dated. It was an embarrassing thing to lie about, but it was a harmless lie, right? What could go wrong?

The girl in the video store lit up. She said, "Oh my god, you know Mandy Clemens? She's one of my best friends. I can't wait to tell her I met you!"

What are the odds? I was all the way across the country. I was mortified and panicked each day at work imagining the moment this girl walked in and I'd have to face her and my lie again. She was so kind that she never came back, but I learned my lesson in trying to look cool:

Don't.

> We often lose access to our natural social skills when we get anxious. That's all the more reason to work on the basics: so you can rely on them consciously when you feel the most triggered.

## The Simplest Social Skills Are the Best

The simplicity principle doesn't just apply to opening lines. After I read the research on conversation starters, I encountered the principle repeatedly. Time and again, I'd be reading studies and the takeaway would be that the simplest and most fundamental social skills were the most important.

I saw this in the wealth of evolutionary psychology research by David Buss, the head honcho of the movement. While his research is ostensibly an effort to support the idea of prominent differences between genders in what they look for in dating partners, what I read sent a different message. Evolutionary folks often conclude that women desire tall men with status and money, and men desire women with youth and beauty. And that may hold some truth, relatively speaking. But focusing on those differences in desired traits downplays the fact that the most important traits to both men and women are basic and achievable. According to one of the Buss studies, here are the top 10 traits each gender wants in a partner:

## What women want in men:
1. Sense of humor
2. Sympathy
3. Good manners
4. Good grooming
5. Willingness to invest his time in her
6. Offers to help her
7. Showers daily
8. Is physically fit
9. Exercises
10. Wears attractive outfits

## What men want in women:
1. Sense of humor
2. Good grooming
3. Sympathy
4. Good manners
5. Showers daily
6. Is physically fit
7. Tells jokes

8. Willingness to invest her time in him
9. Wears attractive outfits
10. Offers to help her

Notice how much overlap there is?

Though we could argue about where each gender *ranked* their top 10 desired traits, the findings can't be dismissed: people generally want simple, achievable social skills in a partner. Overall, we're drawn to those who smile a lot and are warm and kind to others. As we'll discuss later, people *admire* strengths, but we're *drawn* to warmth.

This primacy of the simple shouldn't be too surprising. After all, look at how much mastering the fundamentals of any field contributes to success. Fundamentals are much more important than knowing advanced techniques that are only applicable in certain situations (yet take a lot of practice to master). *They are fundamentals for a reason.*

In social terms, this means becoming solid with the simplest and most effective social skills, without which nothing else will work. I'm not naïve. I know some things you do or say will get a better reaction than others. If you're funny, witty, and talk about interesting things people will respond better than if you say boring, weird, or stupid things. Of course there are such things as advanced social skills. But now is not the time for them (that's something for another book). At this stage, the simple social skills your mother taught you are not only appropriate, they're the preferred method of flirting. This means:

- Make eye contact when someone talks to you
- Smile
- Ask questions
- Answer questions
- Listen
- Introduce yourself to people

If you master these basics—while also doing some basic grooming—you'll be 80 percent of the way there, and I'm not exaggerating one bit.

Don't let great be the enemy of good.

## The Self Presentational Gap

If you knew that starting a conversation was simple and there was no need to be impressive, how would that affect your anxiety? I'm guessing it would be significantly lower and, as a result, you'd be far more likely to engage people. This is a good time for another treatment principle:

*The higher your performance demands,*
*the higher your anxiety.*

And we already know that the higher your anxiety, the more likely you are to avoid social interactions of any kind. To be more precise, the higher your performance expectations are *relative to your belief about how you can perform*, the more anxiety you'll experience. For example, if I tell myself I must appear cool and witty, yet I believe I'll be stuttering and awkward, then I'm going to have a significant amount of anxiety. My performance demands are well above what I believe I can confidently achieve.

This idea grew from the "self presentational model of social anxiety," put forth by psychologists Mark Leary and Robin Kowalski. Whenever I mention this to patients it seems to resonate: the higher your expectations are above what you believe you can achieve—the larger the "self-presentational gap"—the more anxious you get.

## Aim Lower

One of the great problems I notice in my practice is that most people assume the best way to reduce this gap is by increasing performance, such that we achieve our ideal. For example, if I think I must be funny to gain acceptance, then I assume I'll reduce my anxiety by telling funny stories and improving my delivery. This type of solution is reinforced continuously throughout pop culture. People are forever learning to improve themselves in TV shows and movies, and it can be fun to watch.

But this method has serious drawbacks in real life.

One of my patients first came in for treatment having read a whole series of books about how to start conversations with anybody and master the art of witty banter. He desperately wanted to become a great conversationalist—clear, quick on his feet, witty, and funny. But despite all his reading, his anxiety was only getting worse and he was barely talking to anyone. He hoped I'd provide him with a list of new book ideas for improving his social performance.

I told him if he was going to be in treatment with me, I wouldn't make him throw those books away, but he was banned from reading them and certainly banned from acquiring any new ones.

Faced with his incredulity, I asked him to consider why these books hadn't already solved his problem.

"Are you still experiencing anxiety because you don't have enough information? How many self-improvement books do you need to read before you do? Is the tenth book the one that finally gives you the information you need to live up to your performance demands?"

The problem was that his system of improvement couldn't work. Each book actually increased his performance demands—now he had another book's worth of knowledge he was supposed to say and do in order to be good enough. The expectations crept ever upwards. Reading these books felt good in the moment because they promised a performance increase, but they failed in practice because he never performed well enough to meet his escalating expectations. He became so overwhelmed with the lessons he had to remember that he avoided socializing at all. That's when he moved on to the promise of the next book.

Shifting away from this endless cycle of improvement is a significant part of my treatment process. Instead, I suggest you aim lower.

It's difficult, I know. You're thinking, "Oh my god, lower my standards and give up on being the ideal person I want to be!? That would be an insult to my true personality. I'd never settle for less." I sympathize, but if you're reading this book, the demands you have on yourself are almost certainly too high, and that's really working against you. Let me explain.

## The Power of Moderate Stress Levels

In my research and practice with my patients, I came across a very important concept that's illustrated by something called the Yerkes-Dodson graph. It's essentially a model of the relationship between stress and performance. When stress is low, performance is low: "I don't care about the test, therefore I won't study for it," then you do badly. But as stress increases, performance also increases: "I want to do well on this test, so I'll put some effort in," then you do well.

Many people implicitly assume that this trend must continue forever. If a little pressure increases performance a little, then a ton of pressure must increase performance a lot! Wrong.

The Yerkes-Dodson shows us that increasing pressure eventually leads to a decrease in performance. You think, "I have to do well on this test, but I'm not sure I can. Maybe there isn't enough time to study. Everyone's gonna be so mad at me if I fail. This is too stressful, I'm gonna do something else for a while and study later." This is why having high performance demands is such a problem: they cause too much anxiety and trigger a declining performance. Instead, our best performance comes with a *moderate* amount of pressure or stress.

**THE WISDOM OF JUDITH BECK**

Judith Beck, one of the leading proponents of modern cognitive therapy, was being interviewed by a women's magazine about dating. She was asked how people could quell their anxiety before a first date. Her answer was essentially, "Stop trying to make a good impression."

She went on to say:

"What if your goal was just to try to connect with the other person and enjoy yourself? What if you told yourself, 'It's actually okay to be me, as I am, in my natural (perhaps slightly improved) state? I don't have to (overly) impress my date. I just need to show an interest in him/her and talk about myself and things that interest me. Just like I do when I'm out with a friend.'"

To Judith's point, some research shows that people who believe there is a big difference between dating and hanging out with a friend tend to have dating anxiety.

The reporter who was interviewing her seemed a little nonplussed. Apparently, this advice was different from what the interviewer had been reading in magazines.

"But what if you don't look your best and your date, therefore, doesn't want to see you again?" the interviewer asked.

Beck responded with a fantastic line: "Maybe you don't want to date—and potentially end up with—someone so highly judgmental with such perfectionistic standards." The research backs up the exchange between Judith and the interviewer. People usually have a skewed idea of what others value in them as potential partners—this gap between how you perceive your own value and how potential mates value you is called mate value discrepancy. According to a 2005 study by Frederick, Fessler, and Haselton, men in particular tend to overestimate the degree of muscularity that is attractive to women, and women tend to overestimate the degree of thinness that is attractive to men.

## You're Doing Better Than You Think

The truth is, both aspects—your performance demands and how well you believe you can actually perform—should change. We don't need to learn to perform better, *we need to recognize how well we are already doing.* Decrease your demands and increase your belief in yourself. Research shows that people with any social anxiety come across much better than they think, and others rate them much better than they rate themselves.

Those of us with social anxiety tend to engage in overly negative comparisons with others. Also, the research shows that socially anxious people tend to hyperfocus on the negative aspects of their interactions ("I screwed up again, that was so dumb!"), and dismiss the positive ("They were just being nice, but I'm sure on the inside they didn't like me"). They also usually interpret neutral social feedback as negative ("She wasn't all over me, so she must not like me"). This naturally leads to underestimating our social performance. And, as we remember from last chapter, there's also evidence that socially anxious folks make decisions about how social interactions went based on our feelings ("Did I feel anxious or ashamed?") rather than based on observable evidence from the responses of others.

Considering all these biases, is it any wonder we're lacking in social confidence?

### OTHER PEOPLE SCREW UP, TOO

One patient had just gone on an uncomfortable date. His date was closed off and difficult to talk to. She talked about herself, but didn't ask him many questions in response. This is a textbook failure of social skills on her part, and yet he blamed himself, citing his general attractiveness level and his inability to say the right thing to pique her interest. I see this all the time:

> an interaction goes poorly, and rather than seeing
> this as a problem with the other person—or even just
> splitting the burden of responsibility—people blame
> themselves even though their social skills were per-
> fectly appropriate. Just because an interaction doesn't
> go well, doesn't mean you did something wrong.
> Sometimes it's the other person who makes a mistake!

How a conversation goes is not all about you. You could say the same thing to 100 people and get 100 different responses. I might say hi to someone I haven't met yet, and they respond with warmth and friendliness. Then I might say hi to another person, and they pick up their bag and run away like I'm about to abduct them (this actually happened!).

## Do Mediocre Impressions Actually Work?

A famous set of studies revealed that men were more willing than women to have sex with a stranger. This takeaway got a lot of attention, but there's a different finding in these studies that I found far more enlightening. Both genders said "yes" to a date with a stranger who approached them on the street at an astonishingly high rate.

And how impressive were the opening lines that got the dates? Not very. There was little preamble. The initiators were instructed to approach people they liked and say, verbatim, "I've been noticing you around campus. I find you to be very attractive." After they said that, they'd make the date request, "Would you go out with me tonight?"

Astonishingly, half of the people said yes! Across *three* studies and 144 people being asked, 50% of women and 56% of men accepted a date with a stranger.

And these were appealing young college students the initiators actually wanted to date: the study participants rated the people they approached with an average attractiveness rating of 7.5 out of 10.

Whenever I mention these studies to people, they scoff and suggest the initiator must have been very good looking for this to work. There were in fact 20 different initiators (called confederates in research language), so it's not a result of one person who was really good at this. Asking for a date worked in general. And as the original paper says, "The physical attractiveness of both the female and male confederates varied from slightly unattractive to moderately attractive. Ratings of the confederates' attractiveness were found to have no effect on the results."

I don't know about you, but when I was in college I believed that somebody had to be *really* into me before they'd say yes to a date. This led to me failing to ask out many, many women who might have been interested.

I'm not advocating this mass canvassing as your dating strategy (for many reasons, not least of which is that we don't know whether people actually show up for a date after being asked so early in an inter-action). However, I use this study to reinforce the idea that you don't have to be impressive to have a good interaction. You don't have to meet your imagined lofty standards to connect with somebody. Instead, there's reason to believe you can be warm, use simple social skills, and take some reasonable social risks and that's enough to open up a world of dating possibilities.

## The Meet-Cute and Other Myths

Where does this belief come from that we have to be impressive in some way to have somebody like us, or that we have to make a great first impression? I think there are a few answers to this question.

Firstly, there's the meet-cute myth from roman-tic movies which implies that relationships start when idealized attractive strangers connect in a memorable way (often involving witty banter).

Secondly, there are myriad articles, blogs, and social media posts telling us who we must be and what we must do to attract the partner we want. I mean, how many times have you seen a post about "All the things you didn't know are ruining your dating life!" and clicked out of morbid curiosity? These cultural influences only serve to raise our performance demands.

Thirdly, I cannot count the number of times I've been told by patients that the first impression is what really matters. The sentiment goes like this: "If I screw up the first impression, then I screw up the entire relationship. They'll never like me, and the whole thing—which could have been a beautiful fairytale—is now ruined. I'd better avoid talking to them until I've got the perfect thing to say." I get it, this was me in college.

I remember I liked a girl in my music class sophomore year. She was confident, seemed friendly, and was a little nerdy. I knew I had to make a good impression so she'd see me as an attractive guy she wanted to date. But I never felt like I was ready. So I avoided talking to her, going so far as to hide if I saw her around campus. My actions were all based on the belief that how I came across in that initial interaction would make or break my chances of dating her. I kept thinking I could find something better to say if I had more time to think, or I could look better later, or I should be in a more confident state of mind before I talked to her. Of course this never happened and, in the end, I never talked to her.

The truth is it's really not about first impressions. People have this idea that an impression is fixed after the first meeting, and somehow unchangeable. It doesn't work that way. Meeting someone in a social setting isn't a job interview. In the real world, people most commonly connect over time through a series of repeated interactions in which they slowly get to know each other, drop in anxiety, and become more comfortable.

Research shows us that the most important factors in first impressions are:

- Warmth
- Authenticity
- Grooming

These are very achievable standards, don't you think? And notice how similar they are to the top 10 traits people want in a man from earlier in the chapter. Strikingly, one 2011 study found that the single biggest trait linked to positive first impressions was "extensive smiling." (Number two and three were not having a grumpy facial expression, and having a friendly voice tone, all of which I've combined into a trait I call warmth.) And first impressions certainly can change. Multiple studies have shown that narcissists make a great first impression, but within a few meetings become disliked. Why? Because people get to know each other over repeated interactions, and the deeper traits people care about are hard to fake in the long-term.

At its core, the need to be impressive is a monster that emerges directly from the depths of psychological pain. From the heart of anxiety and shame, by way of our self-protection system, the deep belief is: "Who I authentically am is not good enough. I must appear better than I am in order for somebody to love me." Everything grows out of this. If you knew you were good enough, and your goal is simply to find that percentage of people who like you, identify who is a natural fit, and take a shot with them, then how much would you feel the need to create a great impression? You would likely just present yourself authentically and discover the response. The defense of making a great impression is designed to prevent the flawed self from being seen and rejected.

## So What Should We Do Instead?

After you've set your social goals—whether it's talking to five people next time you go out, or consciously focusing on asking more questions of people—make sure they follow the simplicity principle. Don't do anything fancy to reach your social goals, and don't be anything other than what you are (unless, of course, you're playing a bar game for fun). Aim for basic social skills and warmth. Smile, say hi, introduce yourself, show curiosity, and see what happens.

You don't have to do everything at once. Just make a mediocre impression. Do this each time you're in a social situation for a week or two until it becomes a habit. Then you'll start getting natural reinforcement and feedback. Make a mediocre impression both online and in-person and see what happens. Does everyone hate you? Maybe you find that people actually like you more. Don't take my word for it, test it out yourself. See how your life changes.

Next, identify what your *implicit* performance goals are. These are usually very high, idealized images of how you wish to come across. Look for things like: "I must appear..."

- Witty
- Intelligent
- Confident
- Cool
- Anxiety-free
- Funny
- Charismatic

Make these performance demands explicit, so you don't fall prey to them, then deliberately set much lower, simpler, and achievable goals. See what happens when you do.

For example, here's one exercise that's designed to help you with excessive verbal performance demands, which often cause you to filter yourself, because what you have to say is never "good enough." Instead, this exercise requires you to think out loud and see what comes out, with no filtering. What people tend to find is that their anxiety declines because it's a much lower performance goal. Also, their conversations become more natural and less stilted. Rather than making a bad impression, being more open and less protected seems to help them connect more easily.

And when you're talking, make a point of being genuine, authentic, and in the moment. Share your real thoughts, your opinions, and relate your personal experiences. Self-disclose who you are since this is a basic requirement for connection. You don't have to share everything—you'll probably share deeper information the better you get to know somebody—but make sure what you're sharing is true and real. You know those decision points in a conversation when you can choose to reveal more, or you can put on a mask? Choose to reveal who you are in those moments and see what happens. One 1998 study by Alden and Bieling found that people are more likely to enjoy your company not based on how much you talk, but by how revealing you are.

All told, we have no right to control what other people think of us. They are autonomous human beings, with their own reactions and opinions. Like the saying goes, "What other people think of me is none of my business." The more you try to engage in mind control, the more anxious and stressed you'll become. Later on in treatment, people often remark to me how much easier it is to socialize when they're not trying to meet unrealistic performance standards and trying to make other people think certain things about them. Allowing yourself to be friendly and authentic is effective, relaxing, and easy.

## Dropping the James Bond Routine

The better we ask ourselves to perform socially, the more anxious and uncomfortable we're likely to get. Instead, focus on simple social skills, the ones that don't require us to be anything other than mediocre. Smile, say hello, introduce yourself, and express genuine curiosity about the other person. Do those things consistently, and you'll cut off a large chunk of your dating anxiety.

That's how it went for my patient from the beginning of the chapter. He was so focused on saying something impressive that he said nothing at all in social settings. Then we discussed many of the concepts in this chapter. We got him to drop his strong silent routine and focus more on being warm and assertive on his next date.

"How'd your date go?" I asked.

"It was great." He gave a big smile, something he usually didn't do. "I stopped trying to perform, and I was honest with her about myself. And I guess she must've liked me? She was smiling, laughing, and touching me. I made goofy jokes that I always thought made me seem childish, but she laughed at them and was silly in response. The date didn't end until midday the next day. Then we went out again a couple days later."

Even after this happened, I could tell he still didn't fully believe he was safe to drop his cool guy facade. But he agreed that we had one big, convincing piece of evidence.

Hidden in his story is a clue to our next step forward.

He felt the need to perform because he didn't think he was good enough as he was. He saw so many flaws in himself that he assumed other people would criticize and reject him as much as he criticized and rejected himself. Like most of my patients, when he stopped trying to perform, people saw a little more of the real him, and they liked him more.

But what if he revealed more of himself and people rejected him?

It's a scary question, and one that cripples a lot of us with social and dating anxiety. So let's take the next step and figure out what happens if we allow others to see our true, flawed selves: will they hate us or love us?

# Make a Mediocre Impression

## Opening Lines Are Simple: Just Say Something

Best opening lines

Weber, K., Goodboy, A. K., & Cayanus, J. L. (2010). Flirting competence: An experimental study on appropriate and effective opening lines. *Communication Research Reports, 27*(2), 184-191.

Cunningham, M. R. (1989). Reactions to heterosexual opening gambits: Female selectivity and male responsiveness. *Personality and Social Psychology Bulletin, 15*(1), 27–41.

Kleinke, C. L., Meeker, F. B., & Staneski, R. A. (1986). Preference for opening lines: Comparing ratings by men and women. *Sex Roles: A Journal of Research, 15*(11-12), 585–600.

Senko, C., & Fyffe, V. (2010). An evolutionary perspective on effective vs. ineffective pick-up lines. *The Journal of Social Psychology, 150*(6), 648–667.

## Trying to Be Impressive Can Backfire

People respond to honesty better than we expect

Paunonen, S. V. (2006). You are honest, therefore I like you and find you attractive. *Journal of Research in Personality, 40*(3), 237–249.

Levine, E., & Cohen, T.R. (2018). You can handle the truth: Mispredicting the consequences of honest communication. *Journal of Experimental Psychology: General, 147*(9), 1400–1429.

## The Simplest Social Skills Are the Best

People want simple social skills (and achievable traits) in a partner

Buss, D. M. (1988). The evolution of human intrasexual competition: Tactics of mate attraction. *Journal Of Personality and Social Psychology, 54*(4), 616-628.

Buss, D. M. (2007). The evolution of human mating. *Acta Psychologica Sinica, 39*(3), 502–512.

## The Self Presentational Gap

Self-presentational model of social phobia

Leary, M. R., & Kowalski, R. M. (1995). The self-presentational model of social phobia. In R. G. Heimberg, M. R. Liebowitz, D. A. Hope & F. R. Schneier (Eds), *Social Phobia: Diagnosis, Assessment, and Treatment* (pp. 94–112). New York: Guilford Press.

## The Power of Moderate Stress Levels

Yerkes-Dodson graph

Yerkes, R.M., & Dodson, J.D. (1908). The relation of strength of stimulus to rapidity of habit formation. *Journal of Comparative Neurology & Psychology, 18,* 459–482.

## The Wisdom of Judith Beck

Judith Beck article on dating anxiety
Dealing with dating anxiety: Try not to impress, huffpost.com.

We overestimate what dating partners are looking for

Frederick, D. A., Fessler, D. M., & Haselton, M. G. (2005). Do representations of male muscularity differ in men's and women's magazines?. *Body image, 2*(1), 81–86.

## You're Doing Better Than You Think

People with social anxiety have negatively
skewed interpretations and memory

Leary, M. R., & Kowalski, R. M. (1995). The self-presentational model of social phobia. In R. G. Heimberg, M. R. Liebowitz, D. A. Hope & F. R. Schneier (Eds), *Social Phobia: Diagnosis, Assessment, and Treatment* (pp. 94–112). New York: Guilford Press.

Hofmann, S. G., & Otto, M. W. (2018). Chapter 3. *In Cognitive behavioral therapy for social anxiety disorder: Evidence-based and disorder-specific treatment techniques,* Routledge.

Alden, L., & Wallace, S.T. (1995). Social phobia and social appraisal in successful and unsuccessful social interactions. *Behaviour Research and Therapy, 33*(5), 497-505.

Cody, M. W., & Teachman, B. A. (2010). Post-event processing and memory bias for performance feedback in social anxiety. *Journal of Ancient Disorders, 24*(5), 468–479.

## Other People Screw Up Too

People with social anxiety tend to blame themselves

Trower, P., Sherling, G., Beech, J.R., Harrop, C., & Gilbert, P. (1998). The socially anxious perspective in face-to-face interaction: An experimental comparison. *Clinical Psychology & Psychotherapy, 5*(3), 155-166.

## Do Mediocre Impressions Actually Work?

People will accept dates with strangers

Clark, R. D., & Hatfield, E. (1989). Gender differences in receptivity to sexual offers. *Journal of Psychology & Human Sexuality, 2*(1), 39–55.

## The Meet-Cute and Other Myths

Smiling can lead to popularity

Back, M. D., Schmukle, S. C., & Egloff, B. (2011). A closer look at first sight: Social relations lens model analysis of personality and interpersonal attraction at zero acquaintance. *European Journal of Personality, 25*(3), 225-238.

Narcissists often make a good first impression

Back, M. D., Schmukle, S. C., & Egloff, B. (2010). Why are narcissists so charming at first sight? Decoding the narcissism–popularity link at zero acquaintance. *Journal of Personality and Social Psychology, 98*(1), 132-145.

The real qualities people want aren't observable immediately

Hampson, S. E., Goldberg, L. R., & John, O. P. (1987). Category-breadth and social-desirability values for 573 personality terms. *European Journal of Personality, 1*(4), 241–258.

## So What Should We Do Instead?

Self-disclosure leads to increased liking

Collins, N., & Miller, L. (1994). Self-disclosure and liking: A meta-analytic review. *Psychological Bulletin, 116*(3), 457-75.

Alden, L., & Bieling, P. (1998). Interpersonal consequences of the pursuit of safety. *Behaviour Research and Therapy, 36*(1), 53-64.

# CHAPTER 6

. . .

# Allow Yourself to Be Seen, Flaws and All

I was sitting in my office with Javier, a long-term patient. He was slim, bright, passionate, and had the easy charisma of an aspiring actor. He suffered greatly because he was a socially anxious extravert, meaning he craved an unusually full and exciting social life, but was imprisoned by his intense fear of rejection. We worked on many things over the course of treatment, and he'd made great progress in dropping his performance demands, and he started being more authentic. But, as we moved forward, we ran into an anxiety he hadn't disclosed before.

"People won't like me because my teeth are so bad. I know people look at teeth, and they expect your teeth to be perfect and straight. My teeth are terrible. No girls will want to kiss me when they see my teeth. Nothing else will matter if my teeth are this bad."

This was his central "flaw," the most pressing thing about him that he thought wasn't good enough. He truly believed that if people saw his smile, they would reject him. Naturally, he wanted to hide that part of himself.

Sadly, I had to agree with him. "You've got imperfect teeth, and America is obsessed with teeth. If you go to some other countries, it's not such a big deal, but many people in America get braces as teenagers, so I get it."

He looked pretty upset at this point. I continued.

"But I don't agree with your conclusions. We don't *know* that your imperfect teeth lead to disgusted reactions and rejection. We just know that they trigger your fear and avoidance. I believe that you can connect with people even while having imperfect teeth. I had braces for three years in my late twenties. I was really concerned that my dating life would plummet. And yet, it didn't. If anything it improved, though I doubt that was due to having braces.

"At the moment, you can't get rid of your flaw. But you have a lot of influence over how it impacts you and your life. Will it cause you to avoid being friendly and trying to connect? Or will you accept it as part of you? You have bad teeth and that's not about to change anytime soon. So here's your choice: do you want to have bad teeth and be warm and friendly, or do you want to have bad teeth and be cold and isolating?"

There was a long silence as he thought.

I said, "Are you prepared to show your teeth and test this out using some behavioral experiments?"

He gave a sheepish smile for the first time that day and said, "I'm in."

The point of this chapter is that it's okay and safe to be vulnerable and show our authentic, flawed selves. Despite our fears that people won't like us, you'll discover that people will be surprisingly receptive to your inevitable imperfections. If you're willing to take the leap, you'll be able to drastically reduce your anxiety moving forward. Better yet, you'll find it *much* easier to connect. Owning who you are and courageously showing it to others is a very powerful intervention.

## We Think Our Flaws Cause Our Problems

Remember that others see us in total, not our per-ceived flaws in isolation.

Most patients come in believing that flaws are the issue. If only we could get rid of our prob-lems—*I'm too boring, not smart enough, not physically attractive enough, too noticeably nervous*—then we'll be "good enough." But whatever your flaw, I guaran-tee we could find someone with that very same flaw who is socially successful. It doesn't mean your flaw is necessarily likable, just that it doesn't determine social outcomes in the way you imagine.

In fact, this belief—that social struggles are caused by our flaws—is the true heart of the prob-lem. Our attempts to hide our flaws and prevent rejection strongly drive our dating anxiety, and actually cause the rejection we fear. Let me show you what I mean.

## Anxious People Are Less Likable

When most people come to see me they believe their dating or social anxiety makes them less likable. Sadly, they're right. Research (much of it from Dr. Lynn Alden at the University of British Columbia) regularly finds that people with social anxiety are less well-liked during interactions.

So, is it time to quit reading this book and get back to isolating or reading *How to Win Friends and Trick People into Liking You?* Not so fast. We can't simply take that single slice of research at face value. We have to ask why: what is it about social anxiety that makes somebody less likable during social interactions?

One breakthrough in social anxiety treatment came when researchers (lead by Adrian Wells) at the University of Oxford realized that socially anxious people acted in particular ways when socializing. Despite attempts to do exposure therapy—where we face our fears head-on in order to disprove that the situations are dangerous—the researchers observed that people never actually faced their true fears. Instead, when in social situations, they engaged in a series of subtle protective behaviors designed to prevent the outcomes they feared. These became known as "safety behaviors."

Some common safety behaviors are:

- Not revealing anything about yourself for fear of judgment
- Stiffening your face and body to hide signs of nervousness

- Only talking to safe people in social situations
- Not asking questions
- Trying to act confident
- Avoiding eye contact
- Speaking softly or quickly

And, finally, the most common safety behavior: limiting what we say in order to avoid saying the "wrong" thing.

The initial issue with using safety behaviors is that it prevents exposure therapy from working. For example, imagine you're afraid that people will think you're not smart enough. As a result, you filter your words very carefully, to make sure you never say anything that sounds unintelligent. You don't take risks, you think a lot before you speak, and you keep what you say short and to the point, thus keeping your risk of screwing up to a minimum. Can you see how this impedes your exposure to your fears? You'll never get over your fear of speaking freely if you never let yourself speak freely. You never get to find out that what you would say comes across just fine. Instead, you filter yourself greatly, and when nothing goes horribly wrong you think, "That was a close one. I just barely survived thanks to my careful choice of words." This keeps your threat system ready and engaged for next time.

When researchers in these studies prevented people from using safety behaviors, they found a dramatic increase in the effectiveness of treatment. If people truly faced their fears, unprotected, and nothing bad happened, their threat systems finally had a chance to learn that socializing was safe.

## Safety Behaviors Can Look Weird

Safety behaviors do more than maintain anxiety. They can also cause social problems. Firstly, safety behaviors often seem weird—and not in a good way. Safety behaviors are so weird that they sometimes elicit the very reaction they were designed to prevent. For example, to continue our example, maybe you think you're not smart. Instead of filtering yourself, you try to force fancy words into conversation to appear smarter. But because this vocabulary is inauthentic to you, you may use the words incorrectly. As a result, people actually respond worse to you, thus manifesting a self-fulfilling prophecy. Safety behaviors cut off connection. Anxious people *without* safety behaviors are more likable.

**WHATEVER YOU RESIST PERSISTS**

Somebody who worries about sweating might put on extra layers of clothes on to hide it, which inadvertently makes them hot and sweaty. Somebody who worries about shaking might clench their muscles to steady them, which tires them out and leads to more shakiness.

In multiple studies, researchers found that socially anxious people who stop using their safety behaviors are just as well-liked as everyone else.

Think about that.

The problem isn't anxiety. The problem is the defensive behavior our anxiety convinces us to use. When people say "just be yourself" this is what they're referring to: dropping your protective behaviors. People who are open and authentic while experiencing anxiety are actually charismatic. People who attempt to protect themselves are not. To update the quote from Franklin D. Roosevelt: "We have nothing to fear but our self-protective response to fear." Not quite as catchy, but you get the point.

Just remember this: protection is the problem.

## Stop Hiding Your Flaws

What I'm suggesting here likely flies in the face of every piece of dating advice you've come across.

Rather than trying to use surface tricks, tips, and hacks, we're about to tackle dating anxiety on a deep level. Our goal is to turn off your threat system. To do so, we need to break apart what I call the central social anxiety equation.

Our perceived flaws are a core element of the equation that triggers our threat system. As a reminder, here is the series of beliefs that drive social anxiety. You believe:

1. Your perceived flaws will be revealed
2. People will notice your flaws
3. They will also consider them flaws
4. They will be judgmental of your flaws
5. This will lead to harsh rejection
6. The rejection will be unbearable

This string of beliefs is triggered when you imagine entering scary social situations. Each is knocked over in turn, like a row of dominoes, until your threat protection system kicks in and you feel all the traditional social anxiety symptoms. It happens so fast you barely notice it. If we're able to disconfirm any of these beliefs—if we stop one domino from falling—then we can turn off the whole system.

We'll do this by no longer hiding your assumed flaws.

After all, how can you learn that your flaws are acceptable if you constantly suppress them? In order to challenge these beliefs, you have to take a risk. This isn't license to be a jerk or to overcompensate by screaming your insecurities at the top of your lungs. It means you have to be open and authentic. It means dropping your counter-productive, excessive protections and allowing genuine connections.

## The Illusion of Transparency

You might worry that dropping your safety behaviors will backfire. For example, people commonly tell me that if others see their anxiety symptoms they'll be rejected. But what if our flaws aren't as obvious as we think?

There's a phenomenon known as the "illusion of transparency" which I think you should know about. In a series of studies, researchers compared how much anxiety people felt with how anxious they actually appeared to an audience. They found that people believed they came across just as anxious as they felt while making a speech. However, their anxiety *appeared* much lower to the people watching them. The "illusion" was the belief that what they were feeling internally was fully projected externally. But people can't look inside you to see what you're feeling—they can only see what is externally observable. And, it turns out, people perceive significantly less anxiety than what you feel. Why? Because anxiety is a largely internal experience.

Once this illusion of transparency was unearthed, it opened up a world of research (it turns out we believe many things are more observable than they actually are). One study showed that simply informing people about the illusion of transparency before a speech led them to feel more composed and perform better, most likely because it caused people to stop having anxiety about their anxiety. I'd like to quote the study here, because the message is so important:

"So, while you might be so nervous you're convinced that everyone can tell how nervous you are, in reality that's very rarely the case. What's inside of you typically manifests itself too subtly to be detected by others. With this in mind, you should just relax and try to do your best. Know that if you become nervous, you'll probably be the only one to know."

Even better than *telling* yourself nobody can see when you're nervous is *proving* it to yourself. After all, you're the only person who can't observe your-self in social situations. You're forced to rely on your imagination to create a mental picture. And there's a documented tendency for your imaginings about social situations to be unrealistic and negatively skewed (remember mindreading?). A good way to correct self-misperceptions is by fully observing how you come across.

The first step is identifying the flaws you believe you have. You know the ones. It's the thing you're afraid someone will point out if you stop hiding it. One fantastic paper by David Moscovitch suggested that these flaws generally fall into 4 categories:

1. Visible anxiety symptoms
   (e.g., shaky hands)
2. Physical appearance (e.g., acne)
3. Lack of social skills (e.g., nothing to say)
4. Character flaws (e.g., unintelligent)

When you figure out what these flaws are, don't hide in generalities. Get specific. How exactly will your flaws be observable? For example, rather than saying you're nervous about your appear-ance, observe that you're worried "My face will be tomato-red" or "I won't be able to think of answers to questions and will be totally silent." Then think through what your flaw will do to the social interaction. For example, "There will be long, awkward pauses of ten seconds in duration."

The next step is a bit more involved, and more advanced than you may be ready for, but it's incredibly valuable: make small talk with someone and videotape it. Afterward, before you watch the video, rate the intensity of your predicted flaws and how obvious you believe they were. Then watch the video and compare your assumptions to the actual observable evidence from the recording.

This exercise usually rocks people. What you'll almost certainly realize is that you come across completely differently than you imagined. You'll seem friendlier, warmer, more relaxed, and more likable than you assumed. The blushing is not as obvious, the sweating isn't noticeable, the awkward pauses are merely acceptable natural human speech, the shakiness is invisible, and your overall feelings of nervousness and awkwardness are just that: feelings. One patient remarked with astonishment that he looked so normal.

He said, "I came across better than I expected, even the areas where I was certain I came across badly. Even when I was at my worst and thought my anxiety was most apparent, I still didn't seem that way—I thought I was pausing and stumbling over my words. But on the video, it just looks like I was collecting my thoughts."

This exercise—which I first learned about from reading Stefan Hofmann's work—typically leads to a distinct drop in anxiety over the proceeding few weeks. There is a stark, shocking contrast between the mental picture we have of ourselves and what we can actually see on camera as an impartial observer. Once we learn that feeling like we're flawed doesn't mean people see a flaw, we can stop focusing on it as much. Then it gets much easier to externalize our attention and socialize.

## It Makes You Raise an Eyebrow

So why do we imagine our flaws are so much worse and more obvious than they appear? It has a lot to do with a factor we discussed earlier: the power of attention.

I recently realized I had thinner eyebrows than in my youth, and wondered if they were getting too thin. I had given almost no thought in my life to eyebrows up to this point. But I found myself becoming aware of everyone's eyebrow thickness and length. I noticed that some people had incredibly thick eyebrows and some had almost none at all. Some started thick in the middle and thinned out by the edge. I noticed and began to form opinions on what I considered good and bad eyebrows. I regularly checked and critiqued mine and imagined the problems that my thinning eyebrows would cause. I went from paying no attention to eyebrows to focusing on them a ton. Meanwhile, the belief that other people noticed and cared about my eyebrows escalated dramatically. My anxiety did the same.

I knew I had to intervene in this runaway process. I forced myself to stop checking my eyebrows multiple times a day and to stop analyzing everyone else's. I also did some exposures where I stared at my eyebrows without looking away for a long time until I got bored. By doing this, my anxiety dropped again and I fell back into my previous position of hardly even being aware of eyebrows. And again I came to assume my eyebrows were fine. Not ideal, but acceptable.

When we focus on our flaw, it gets bigger and brighter in our perceptions. Other people observing us are aware of the whole picture—they might see our flaw (if it's even noticeable or significant at all), but they'll see it simply as one piece of a larger puzzle. There's so much new information to take in when we come across a new person that focusing on one thing is very rare.

This is why it's hard to remember someone's name when you first meet them: there are simply too many stimuli to latch onto one thing.

In the absence of clear, overt evidence, we fill in the gaps with our negatively skewed assumptions.

In a remarkable study from the 80's, researchers explored different aspects of prejudice. Some subjects were given an obvious stigmatized flaw: makeup artists created the illusion of a large scar on their faces. Then these "disfigured" subjects were introduced to other subjects to see the reactions. The study designers compared the perceptions of the people with the fake scars on their faces and a control group. Compared to the control group, the "disfigured" subjects believed other people liked them less, were more tense, and more distanced from them.

However, the study had a twist. Right before the participants were sent out, the makeup artists explained that they needed to moisturize the scar to stop it from cracking. The makeup artists then removed the scar without the participants realizing it. That meant something shocking: the subjects who thought they were "disfigured" looked like their normal selves. The reactions those participants perceived in others couldn't have been influenced by the scar because the scar wasn't there! The study authors put it really well:

"Subjects presumably entered the experiment anticipating how others might respond to various forms of physical deviance and, when placed in interaction with a peer, readily found evidence consistent with these expectations."

In other words, we see what we expect to see. If we think our flaw leads to rejection, rejection is what we'll experience. Perhaps we interpret neutral responses as negative, or maybe we elicit negative responses with our protective responses.

## "What Did They Think of You?"

Now, I know you may be so convinced of your flaws that it feels like this doesn't apply to you. I get that. Maybe every time something goes wrong socially, you *know* that it's due to your flaws. But take a second to question whether you have clear, concrete, direct evidence that anyone even notices your flaw, let alone cares. Remember, this is one of those areas where we are strongly biased.

This is referred to as meta-accuracy: the degree to which we have an accurate understanding of how we are seen. Most research suggests that we don't fully trust external feedback from other people—we focus on our internal perceptions and assumptions.

There are many studies that have tested people's meta-accuracy. Some studies set up fast-paced two-person interactions between men and women, similar to speed dating. Then the researchers compare the person's perception of how the interactions went to what their interaction partner actually said about them. The results of these studies tend to show that there's little correlation. In other words, how the person believed they came across was largely unrelated to what their partner actually thought. Why? Because nobody has access to the private thoughts of others, and when we fill in the blanks with our own beliefs and projections, we often get it wrong.

But here's an extra piece of *very* important information. In most meta-accuracy studies, there's a strong connection between what people believe others think about them, and what they think about themselves. Take a second to consider this. For example, if you believe you're awkward, you're very likely to assume others think you're awkward too.

But most studies show that the people you meet are unlikely to think this. When we think we're reading someone's mind, we are merely reading our own thoughts and projecting them onto others. There's a tendency in people who experience social anxiety, depression, and low self-esteem to underestimate how positively we're viewed by others.

But, again, what if people *do* observe our flaws? Your weird earlobes, lack of charisma, awkwardness, stuttering, or thinning hair can't all be invisible... right? I once took a patient out to do a series of behavioral experiments to test this very question.

## People Like Openness More Than They Dislike Flaws

Daniel was a successful professional in his thirties and he was doing great in treatment. He was smart, very likable, and had a young Tom Hanks feel about him. But he was a little socially perfectionistic. He had a strong aversion to showing weaknesses, or making any mistakes.

So we went out with the goal of revealing flaws and vulnerabilities to see what really happened. We went to a pharmacy and Daniel asked for help from the cashier. He told her about his hemorrhoids, and asked about the best treatment. He expected revulsion or condemnation, but instead we got a neutral professional response. He was shocked but assumed it was a fluke. To his great surprise, when he asked someone at Walmart for help with enemas, he didn't get derision. Instead, the shop attendant talked about his own use of the products, and which ones helped him with his problems. This was quite unexpected for Daniel.

We pushed things a little further at the next store. Daniel asked for extra-small condoms, telling the shop attendants that the normal sizes were too big. Once again, people surprised us with their humanity. They took turns speaking with us, trying to figure out a good solution. One store clerk mentioned a supplement he used to increase the girth of his penis. I probably don't need to point out that this level of shared vulnerability is an unusual experience in a retail setting. But by openly discussing a "flaw" or making a social "mistake," Daniel found that other people were more likely to reciprocate with openness of their own rather than criticize him.

> Daniel later told me this was the most effective session in his treatment, but part of me did feel like we had tricked caring people into revealing themselves on false pretenses.

The takeaway was clear: despite your fears, being vulnerable is more likely to be reciprocated than judged harshly.

We are all human, and we're all flawed. You're not alone: most of us fear that revealing our perceived flaws will lead to judgment and rejection. But doesn't it feel so much easier to be authentic when the other person does it first?

## We Love Flawed People

One of my all-time favorite studies helps explain the conundrum of why people like us more if we reveal our weaknesses. Because, on the surface, that idea just sounds wrong. If we reveal our negative characteristics, people should like us *less*, not more. That's the basic premise behind using safety behaviors in the first place.

So researchers asked one group of study subjects to reveal their fears, insecurities, and other negative traits. Some examples were:

- I often keep my opinions to myself for fear that others will judge me negatively.
- I'm overly critical of myself and often feel inadequate around others.

- I can be closed-minded to ideas and opinions that are unlike my own.
- I can be extremely impulsive and often regret the decisions I make.
- I get frustrated easily and tend to give up on things before I should.

The researchers then asked the participants to express their positive traits, for example:

- I express my opinions openly rather than worrying about how others will judge me.
- I am pretty secure in who I am.
- I am open to new ideas and opinions that are unlike my own.
- I am level-headed and good at keeping my cool when making tough decisions.
- I don't give up, and always try to see things through to the end.

Once the participants disclosed this information, the researchers told them it would be revealed to an audience, who would then rate what they thought about each participant, and how much they liked them. More specifically, the audience would rate whether they liked the study participants in a friendly or romantic context. But there was a twist: some lucky participants would only have to reveal their positive and neutral traits to the audience. The rest of the unlucky chumps in the study would have to reveal their negative traits to the audience.

Obviously, the people in the weaknesses group freaked out about how badly people would think of them. But the results were very different than you might expect: the audience liked the people who revealed insecurities and vulnerabilities more than they liked those who expressed strengths. Crazy, right?

### EMBARRASSMENT = COOPERATION

This isn't the only time something like this has come up in the research. There is a whole slew of studies showing that if you embarrass people, they are actually better liked. In fact, blushing has been shown to lead to being better liked after a social transgression. This doesn't fit with our assumptions that we need to appear awesome, perfect, and flawless. The evolutionary theory is that an appropriately embarrassed response, such as blushing, shows that we're engaged with the group, we care about the opinions of others, and we're willing to work for the good of the group. On some level, embarrassment makes us seem more open to connection.

The audience preferred people who revealed weaknesses over those who only showed strengths. Why? Do people prefer weaknesses to strengths? Luckily, the researchers dug a little deeper. They asked the audience not only for their ratings, but they also asked *why* they gave particular ratings. The answer wasn't that people inherently like weaknesses and failures. It turns out that while people dislike weaknesses, we *really* like:

- Honesty
- Genuineness
- Openness

Revealing flaws signals openness and honesty. Therefore, people interpreted the choice to reveal flaws to be so appealing that it more than made up for the negative content itself.

Revealing your flaws makes it much easier for people to connect with you. By creating that space in the interaction, the other person is more likely to risk revealing their own imperfections. Your bravery in revealing your flaws, therefore, allows both of you to be more human with each other. Personally, I love it when I meet somebody who's open about their vulnerabilities. It takes a lot of pressure off me to seem perfect and it makes me less worried they'll judge me.

I remember interacting with my program director in the college counseling center during my psychology training. I was always intimidated and stilted when I talked to her. Then she opened up about a struggle she was having with a patient. I instantly felt my stress drop. No authority figure had ever revealed this kind of insecurity in my academic career. They always conveyed this all-knowing aura, and the same was expected of me. I felt a sense of relief at being allowed to show the real me in that environment.

## Hiding Your Flaws Is the Real Flaw

Half of the connection process is just revealing something about yourself. Without revealing who you are, the other person has nothing to connect to. Research shows that people like us more when we self-disclose to them. Moreover, they are more likely to think we're similar to each other after we've self-disclosed. Think about it. How many friendships of yours have fizzled or failed to deepen because your friend was unable to reveal much about themselves beyond the surface level? If you're like me, at least a few. On the other hand, in my experience, the closest friends are very open.

One example of how hiding your flaws can actively prevent connection is by looking at the most powerful and basic connection behavior: smiling. If you don't smile, you'll find it exceedingly difficult to connect with anybody, especially romantically. It's the most obvious indication of warmth, and people innately respond very strongly to it. For example, babies can't really do anything except eat, poop, and smile (which they can do as early as six weeks old). It's not a huge exaggeration to say that their ability to smile is their only survival method. Look at the best-loved people, and the people with the most friends, and you'll find they're likely big smilers. One study looking at interpersonal attraction found that the single biggest predictor of liking someone on first meetings was something they termed "extensive smiling."

And yet, many people cut off this most powerful channel of connection due to perceived flaws. My patient from the beginning of the chapter didn't smile due to a belief that other people would reject him because of his teeth. Another patient refused to smile because he believed his face looked more appealing when it was blank. One patient feared that smiling would encourage people to keep talking to her, increasing the chance she would say something stupid. Yet another believed that he came across weak and childlike when he smiled, so he clenched his jaw and frowned to compensate with a display of strength and gravitas. Even I smiled less when I wanted to hide the facial shakiness that often came with my anxiety.

How many other ways might we be cutting off connection in an effort to hide a flaw?

## The Relief of Being Open

It's so much less stressful and anxiety-provoking to interact with people honestly and openly. One of my patients worked hard to be more open and self-disclosing. In the middle of treatment, he told me about an interaction he had with a coworker he thought was cute, but never talked to. When my patient talked to her, she told him he was far different than she assumed in the past.

"You were so quiet and distant. But now that we're talking I feel way more connected to you than I expected."

Then she asked him out, which never would have happened if he hadn't been open with her.

In order to find out that we're acceptable, we need to show ourselves, risk rejection, and give other people a chance to let us know that we're good enough. If you never take that risk, consider how it traps you: if you never show people your true self, you'll never learn that your true self is acceptable. And because you never discover that, your threat system always feels the need to protect you. Thus you only get more anxious over time as you acquire more and more apparent evidence that you're unacceptable due to your self-induced social isolation and avoidance.

The saddest part is that self-protection prevents us from learning the deepest lesson of all, and the one at the heart of all our suffering: we are good enough and we are lovable as we are, flaws and all.

## How We Cut Off the Connections We Crave

Back when I was very young and desperate for answers, and unsure where to find them, I slipped into the work of Pickup Artists. I didn't realize it at the time, but that entire community was made up of people developing evermore elaborate systems of safety behaviors to keep them from revealing their true selves (everything down to the fake names). Sometimes these people *performed* better romantically than they did previously, but most of them didn't get better *internally*. They weren't actually fixing their problems, they were just making more and more desperate attempts to cover them up, while often hurting others as well as themselves.

I remember reading a post years ago from one of the most famous Pickup Artists at the time. He described how depressed he was after he put all this work into learning how to come across as someone women would like. Although it worked for him, the success never raised his authentic self-esteem because he knew that women liked his techniques, but nobody actually liked *him*. At our core, being seen and being loved is what we really want. And without being known, accepted, and loved for who we are, we will never be satisfied, no matter how many people we date.

> Imagine how good it would feel to drop all of your protections and be your complete self. And once you do that, to realize that people can love you and care about you even though you're anxious, you sometimes use the wrong words, and you're sometimes not very interesting. How might your life change then?

## Are You Living as Though You're Fifteen?

One patient said something very enlightening as I

was writing this book. He said, "If I drop my guard or I'm vulnerable, people will use it against me." This belief led him to be very defensive socially, even as he yearned to connect deeply with people. His belief (and his coping method) made total sense when I discovered that he was bullied by his classmates through middle school and high school. But when he came to treatment he was thirty-eight, and the bullying had ended twenty years earlier. Why was his belief system still active and controlling his behavior? He asked me the same thing.

The answer was that he never gave his beliefs a chance to be updated.

He's far from alone. Many people who come to see me eventually realize that they're operating on beliefs that are based on how their social world worked in childhood. The adult world operates very differently. The percentage of jerks and bullies drops significantly after high school, but you'd never find this out if you're not willing to take a risk.

There's no evidence to suggest people like using your openness against you. Just the opposite. We're all flawed, and deep down we know it. Nobody is so intelligent that they have no more to learn, nobody is so good-looking that they can't point out problem areas they're insecure about, and nobody is so confident that they never feel uncertain. We are all human.

> ### CHANG AND ENG BUNKER
>
> Whatever your flaw, I guarantee we could find someone with that very same flaw who is socially successful.
>
> Let's consider the case of Chang and Eng Bunker, the conjoined twins who spawned the phrase Siamese twins. They moved to America from modern-day Thailand in the mid-1800's, at a time when the culture was particularly racist against Asians. And yet, Chang and Eng found a pair of American sisters (Sarah and Adelaide Yates) who they fell in love with and married. Between the two couples, Chang and Eng fathered 21 children.
>
> So when you tell yourself you're too short, old, boring, unattractive, bald, or awkward to date, just remember the challenges faced by Chang and Eng. They were attached at the sternum, shared a liver, and still found love. Their story reminds us that there is a fit out there for all of us.

## What's Your Strategy?

Let's go over some common protective strategies that people use to hide their flaws and insecurities. Which of these do you use?

- Avoiding eye contact
- Controlling your facial expression or body language

- Taking two shots before going out socially
- Only talking to people you know
- Avoiding conversations with people you find attractive
- Hiding your shaky hands
- Carefully filtering your speech to say only the right thing
- Limiting what you say as much as possible
- Hiding your thoughts or opinions that people may not agree with
- Agreeing with somebody even when what they're saying isn't true
- Concealing any indications of anxiety
- Practicing what to say or how to behave in advance

When you've identified your protective strategies, ask yourself what you're protecting yourself from. What flaw do you worry would be revealed about you? Some of the most common ones I hear are: appearing unintelligent, low status, socially incompetent, boring, annoying, uninteresting, weak, and anxious.

Want to go a layer deeper? Ask yourself when and where you developed this belief and the subsequent coping response. Often, it was learned a long time ago. Do you know for certain that it's still helpful?

Next, take the risk to test out your anxious belief. Allow your weaknesses to be revealed, maybe to somebody really safe at first, and see how they respond. When I started doing this, it began with being more open and honest about my thoughts, opinions, and vulnerabilities with close friends, all of whom were very supportive. It became easier over time to become more authentic with strangers, including women I was attracted to.

Once you realize that you don't have to hide, and that who you naturally are is acceptable, it's a really wonderful feeling. You get a view of the Warm Social World that the least lonely people know. My patients often remark how much easier it is to interact without the layers of safety behaviors and self-focused analysis. Suddenly, socializing is easy and fun.

## Smiling Through the Pain

I was talking with my client who was insecure about his imperfect teeth.

"Your homework is to videotape yourself talking and smiling. Then watch the video to allow yourself to get used to your teeth. Next, go smile at everybody for the next week. Let's find out just how critical people are about your teeth. Then we'll come back and see how it went."

He did his homework as planned, and we set increasingly difficult goals as the weeks went on. As he smiled more, people reciprocated his warmth, and he had better interactions and conversations.

By the end, he came to a wonderful conclusion: "People care about warmth more than they care about teeth."

As he moved through the exposures and behavioral experiments, he gained more confidence. So much confidence that he started a YouTube channel. He did live videos, and he amassed subscribers and followers, some of whom became friends and romantic partners—all while smiling with his imperfect teeth.

We must accept our authentic selves, flaws and all. Not just because it's good for our emotional well-being, but because there's no other option. If you wait to be your true self until you've gotten rid of all your flaws, you'll wait until you're dead.

So own who you are. Embrace your quirks—
these are what make you lovable. So be flawed and
friendly. Be anxious and friendly, short and friendly,
or bald and friendly. Once you're open about who
you are, the next step is taking romantic risks. The
first of which is signaling your interest.

# CHAPTER 6 REFERENCES

# Allow Yourself to Be Seen, Flaws and All

## We Think Our Flaws Cause Our Problems

People do not see our flaws in isolation

Savitsky, K., Epley, N., & Gilovich, T. (2001). Do others judge us as harshly as we think? Overestimating the impact of our failures, shortcomings, and mishaps. *Journal of Personality and Social Psychology, 81*(1), 44–56.

## Anxious People Are Less Likable

People with social anxiety are less well liked by others

Günak, M. M., Clark, D. M., & Lommen, M. (2020). Disrupted joint action accounts for reduced likability of socially anxious individuals. *Journal of Behavior Therapy and Experimental Psychiatry, 68*, 101512.

Alden, L., & Wallace, S.T. (1995). Social phobia and social appraisal in successful and unsuccessful social interactions. *Behaviour Research and Therapy, 33*(5), 497-505.

Voncken, M., Alden, L., Bögels, S., & Roelofs, J. (2008). Social rejection in social anxiety disorder: The role of performance deficits, evoked negative emotions and dissimilarity. *The British Journal of Clinical Psychology, 47*(Pt 4), 439-50.

Socially anxious people use safety behaviors

Wells, A., Clark, D.M., Salkovskis, P.M., Ludgate, J.W., Hackmann, A., & Gelder, M.G. (2016). Social phobia: The role of in-situation safety behaviors in maintaining anxiety and negative beliefs—Republished Article. *Behavior Therapy, 47*(5), 669-674.

Exposures dropping safety behaviors are
more effective in treating social anxiety

Clark, D. M., & Wells, A. (1995). A cognitive model of social phobia. In R. G. Heimberg, M. R. Liebowitz, D. A. Hope, & F. R. Schneier (Eds.), *Social phobia: Diagnosis, assessment, and treatment* (p. 69–93). The Guilford Press.

Morgan, H., & Raffle, C. (1999). Does reducing safety behaviours improve treatment response in patients with social phobia? *Australian and New Zealand Journal of Psychiatry, 33*(4), 503-510.

Dropping safety behaviors encourages
social approach behavior

Taylor, C. T., & Alden, L. E. (2011). To see ourselves as others see us: An experimental integration of the intra and interpersonal consequences of self-protection in social anxiety disorder. *Journal of Abnormal Psychology, 120*(1), 129–141.

Wells, A., Clark, D.M., Salkovskis, P.M., Ludgate, J.W., Hackmann, A., & Gelder, M.G. (2016). Social phobia: The role of in-situation safety behaviors in maintaining anxiety and negative beliefs—Republished Article. *Behavior Therapy, 47*(5), 669-674.

Voncken, M. J., Alden, L. E., & Bögels, S. M. (2006). Hiding anxiety versus acknowledgment of anxiety in social interaction: Relationship with social anxiety. *Behaviour Research and Therapy, 44*(11), 1673-9.

## Safety Behaviors Look Weird

Safety behaviors can impede social performance

Rowa, K., Paulitzki, J.R., Ierullo, M.D., Chiang, B., Antony, M., McCabe, R., & Moscovitch, D. (2015). A false sense of security: Safety behaviors erode objective speech performance in individuals with social anxiety disorder. *Behavior Therapy, 46*(3), 304-14.

Stangier, U., Heidenreich, T., & Schermelleh-Engel, K. (2006). Safety behaviors and social performance in patients with generalized social phobia. *Journal of Cognitive Psychotherapy, 20*(1), 17–31.

Stevens, S., Hofmann, M., Kiko, S., Mall, A., Steil, R., Bohus, M., & Hermann, C. (2010). What determines observer-rated social performance in individuals with social anxiety disorder? *Journal of Anxiety Disorders, 24*(8), 830-6.

Those who used safety behaviors were
judged more negatively by others
Alden, L., & Bieling, P. (1998). Interpersonal consequences of the pursuit of safety. *Behaviour Research and Therapy, 36*(1), 53-64.

Salkovskis, P. M. (1991). The importance of behaviour in the maintenance of anxiety and panic: A cognitive account. *Behavioural Psychotherapy, 19*(1), 6–19.

Wells, A., Clark, D.M., Salkovskis, P.M., Ludgate, J.W., Hackmann, A., & Gelder, M.G. (2016). Social phobia: The role of in-situation safety behaviors in maintaining anxiety and negative beliefs—Republished Article. *Behavior Therapy, 47*(5), 669-674.

Papsdorf, M., & Alden, L. (1998). Mediators of social rejection in social anxiety: Similarity, self-disclosure, and over signs of anxiety. *Journal of Research in Personality, 32*(3), 351-369.

Reducing safety behaviors leads to better interactions
Alden, L., & Bieling, P. (1998). Interpersonal consequences of the pursuit of safety. *Behaviour Research and Therapy, 36*(1), 53-64.

Curtis, R. C., & Miller, K. (1986). Believing another likes or dislikes you: Behaviors making the beliefs come true. *Journal of Personality and Social Psychology, 51*(2), 284–290.

Stinson, D.A., Cameron, J.J., Wood, J.V., Gaucher, D., & Holmes, J.G. (2009). Deconstructing the "reign of error": Interpersonal warmth explains the self-fulfilling prophecy of anticipated acceptance. *Personality and Social Psychology Bulletin, 35*(9), 1165-1178.

## The Illusion of Transparency

Core articles on the illusion of transparency

Gilovich, T., & Savitsky, K. (1999). The Spotlight Effect and the illusion of transparency. *Current Directions in Psychological Science, 8*(6), 165-168.

Savitsky, K., & Gilovich, T. (2003). The illusion of transparency and the alleviation of speech anxiety. *Journal of Experimental Social Psychology, 39*(6), 618-625.

What we think others see in us is actually what we see in ourselves

Christensen, P.N., Stein, M., & Means-Christensen, A. (2003). Social anxiety and interpersonal perception: A social relations model analysis. *Behaviour Research and Therapy, 41*(11), 1355-71.

Chambers, J. R., Epley, N., Savitsky, K., & Windschitl, P. D. (2008). Knowing too much. *Psychological Science, 19*(6), 542-548.

The four types of socially anxious flaws

Moscovitch, D. A. (2009). What is the core fear in social phobia? A new model to facilitate individualized case conceptualization and treatment. *Cognitive and Behavioral Practice, 16*(2), 123–134.

Using video feedback to correct distorted perceptions

Hofmann, S. G., & Otto, M. W. (2018). Chapter 4. *In Cognitive behavioral therapy for social anxiety disorder: Evidence-based and disorder-specific treatment techniques*, Routledge.

Warnock-Parkes, E., Wild, J., Stott, R., Grey, N., Ehlers, A., & Clark, D. M. (2017). Seeing is believing: Using video feedback in cognitive therapy for social anxiety disorder. *Cognitive and Behavioral Practice, 24*(2), 245–255.

## It Makes You Raise an Eyebrow

People do not see our flaws in isolation

Savitsky, K., Epley, N., & Gilovich, T. (2001). Do others judge us as harshly as we think? Overestimating the impact of our failures, shortcomings, and mishaps. *Journal of Personality and Social Psychology, 81*(1), 44–56.

Fake scar study

Kleck, R. E., & Strenta, A. (1980). Perceptions of the impact of negatively valued physical characteristics on social interaction. *Journal of Personality and Social Psychology, 39*(5), 861–873.

## "What Did She Think of You?"

Meta-accuracy—we are often wrong about how others see us

Allik, J., Realo, A., Mõttus, R., Borkenau, P., Kuppens, P., & Hřebíčková, M. (2010). How people see others is different from how people see themselves: A replicable pattern across cultures. *Journal of Personality and Social Psychology, 99*(5), 870–882.

Back, M., Penke, L., Schmukle, S., & Asendorpf, J. (2011). Knowing your own mate value. *Psychological Science, 22*(8), 984-989.

Kenny, D. A., & DePaulo, B. M. (1993). Do people know how others view them? An empirical and theoretical account. *Psychological Bulletin, 114*(1), 145–161.

We are seen as better than we expect, especially if we have social anxiety or depression

Tissera, H., Gazzard Kerr, L., Carlson, E. N., & Human, L. J. (2021). Social anxiety and liking: Towards understanding the role of metaperceptions in first impressions. *Journal of Personality and Social Psychology, 121*(4), 948–968.

Boothby, E. J., Cooney, G., Sandstrom, G. M., & Clark, M. S. (2018). The liking gap in conversations: Do people like us more than we think? *Psychological Science, 29*(11), 1742–1756.

Moritz, D., & Roberts, J. E. (2018). Self-other agreement and metaperception accuracy across the big five: Examining the roles of depression and self-esteem. *Journal of Personality, 86*(2), 296–307.

## We Love Flawed People

People generally like it when you are honest, vulnerable, or reveal your flaws

Gromet, D. M., & Pronin, E. (2009). What were you worried about? Actors' concerns about revealing fears and insecurities relative to observers' reactions. *Self and Identity, 8*(4), 342–364.

Bruk, A., Scholl, S., & Bless, H. (2018). Beautiful mess effect: Self-Other differences in evaluation of showing vulnerability. *Journal of Personality and Social Psychology, 115*(2), 192–205.

Levine, E., & Cohen, T.R. (2018). You can handle the truth: Mispredicting the consequences of honest communication. *Journal of Experimental Psychology: General, 147*(9), 1400–1429.

The positive social aspects of embarrassment and blushing

Keltner, D., & Anderson, C. (2000). Saving face for Darwin: The functions and uses of embarrassment. *Current Directions in Psychological Science, 9*(6), 187–192.

Montoya, R. M., & Horton, R. S. (2014). A two-dimensional model for the study of interpersonal attraction. *Personality and Social Psychology Review, 18*(1), 59–86.

Dijk, C., de Jong, P. J., & Peters, M. L. (2009). The remedial value of blushing in the context of transgressions and mishaps. *Emotion, 9*(2), 287–291.

## Hiding Your Flaws Is the Real Flaw

We like others, and they like us,
when we self-disclose to them

Collins, N. L., & Miller, L. C. (1994). Self-disclosure and liking: A meta-analytic review. *Psychological Bulletin, 116*(3), 457–475.

Sprecher, S., Treger, S., & Wondra, J. D. (2013). Effects of self-disclosure role on liking, closeness, and other impressions in get-acquainted interactions. *Journal of Social and Personal Relationships, 30*(4), 497–514.

Stevens, S., Hofmann, M., Kiko, S., Mall, A. K., Steil, R., Bohus, M., & Hermann, C. (2010). What determines observer-rated social performance in individuals with social anxiety disorder? *Journal of Anxiety Disorders, 24*(8), 830–836.

Being open can lead others to be open

Sprecher, S., Treger, S., Wondra, J. D., Hilaire, N., & Wallpe, K. (2013). Taking turns: Reciprocal self-disclosure promotes liking in initial interactions. *Journal of Experimental Social Psychology, 49*(5), 860–866.

The costs of not disclosing

Baum, S. M., & Critcher, C. R. (2020). The costs of not disclosing. *Current Opinion in Psychology, 31,* 72–75.

The power of smiling

Sprecher, S., Wenzel, A., & Harvey, J. H. (2008). Handbook of relationship initiation. New York: Psychology Press.

Otta, E., Lira, B. B., Delevati, N. M., Cesar, O. P., & Pires, C. S. (1994). The effect of smiling and of head tilting on person perception. *The Journal of Psychology, 128*(3), 323–331.

CHAPTER 7

. . .

# Show Your Interest

One of my patients was having a great time at a house party. He was happily joking around with a group of people, but whenever the girl he found attractive entered the group, he suddenly shut down. He went from talkative to quiet. No more laughing, no more jokes, no more playfulness.

Whenever she left, he perked up again and became his usual social self. As we explored in treatment, we realized that his defenses kicked in whenever she was present. Why? Because he worried she could tell he liked her. Rather than letting these feelings flow naturally and be observable to her, he clenched down against them. These feelings would have likely made him more energetic, more smiley, and more willing to engage with her. But he was afraid of this, so he said nothing. At some point he realized she'd left the party, and he'd never even talked to her.

It can bring up anxiety, and it seems risky, but you can't develop relationships unless you show your attraction. Hiding your interest is one of the major safety behaviors in dating anxiety. In this chapter, we'll talk about the ways suppressing attraction cuts off connection, and how being more obvious with romantic interest helps to escalate reciprocation. If you get this part down, your anxiety will improve, and the number of dates you go on will increase drastically.

## Feigning Disinterest Doesn't Create Connection

One of my other patients struggled talking to a girl he liked. He wanted to get to know her while also hiding the fact that he was attracted to her.

"Why are you hiding that?" I asked him.

"Girls don't like it if you're into them."

"Explain."

"Well, if you're into them, they get creeped out and think you're weak or not cool enough. People always want what they can't have."

"So this means you have to get closer to someone, talk with them, ask them out, go out on dates, and connect, but you need to do all this while acting like you're not interested? Your theory is that if you communicate that you don't like a girl, she'll become more into you until you're a couple?"

"Yes."

"How does anybody start dating if that's the case? How would you ever kiss a girl without showing you liked her? How do you move closer while backing away? Wouldn't everyone just be avoiding each other?"

He didn't have an answer. It would take more work to drop his "too cool to care" act, but we got there eventually. There is some element of truth to the idea that people want what they can't have, but it's a common misconception that people *only* want what they can't have.

Flirtation inherently involves ambiguity, plausible deniability, and the mix of encouraging and discouraging signals. When someone hints that they're interested but we're not sure, it makes us want to complete the circle and get confirmation that they are.

To be very clear, flirtation isn't about sending nonstop "get away from me" signals. It has more to do with mixed signals. You mix in a ton of warmth and encouragement along the way. If you're reading this book, it's likely that your avoidance and discouragement signals are already working. That's why I encourage you to work on the other end of the flirtation equation: showing direct interest. As you improve your encouraging signals, you'll find a nice balance—and that's where the magic is.

## Trying to Show More Interest

When I lived in Boston, I had a friend named Brett who was working as a bartender part-time while studying to be a doctor. Though he was likable, he'd been single for quite a long time, and struggled with dating. I told him if he made his interest more obvious, a significant percentage of women would reciprocate.

"I don't know," he said.

"Let's test it out!" I said, as I always do.

I challenged him to make eye contact with every woman he found attractive. His normal instinct was to look at women he liked, then quickly look away feigning disinterest. But not tonight. A woman walked past, and he looked at her intensely with a big frown on his face.

"How was that?" he said.

"Well, were you trying to make her feel horrible about herself? She's probably thinking, 'That guy looked at me and thought I'm not good enough. What's wrong with me?'"

He paused. "I've never thought about it like that before."

Another girl walked past. He made eye contact, smiled, and she did a double take, even though she was with a guy. The next girl he made eye contact with froze for a second and smiled back. He was making great progress.

But dating anxiety is insidious, and it has myriad ways of creeping back. Brett went up to the bar to get another round. A couple of girls we'd noticed earlier were standing nearby. He overheard them order tequila shots. When Brett ordered our drinks, he paid for the girls' shots. Perfect—buying someone a drink is a classic signal of interest. But then, instead of turning to talk to them, he took his drinks and came back to our table.

He told me what happened and I made fun of him.

Just as he was responding, the girls came up to us, smiling.

"Hey, the bartender told us you bought our drinks. Thanks."

Brett said, "Yeah, don't worry about it," and started looking at his phone. His behavior gave every indication of being uninterested and possibly annoyed that they'd bothered him. After leaving our table, I noticed they left the bar.

They went through all the trouble of breaking gender norms, came all the way across the room to find him and start a conversation, and he basically said, "I'm not interested, now go away." Even though he was interested! What exactly was going on? In short, Brett was hiding his attraction. And it was sabotaging his dating life.

## Common Ways of Hiding Attraction

Besides ignoring the person you like, here are some common ways I see people hiding their attraction:

- Looking at the person you like, then quickly looking away if they make eye contact.
- Deliberately not talking to the person you find attractive.
- Trying to seem like you're only platonically interested in someone.
- Not smiling or making eye contact with them as much as you naturally want to.

- Clamping down on your behavior so they can't tell you're interested.
- Waiting for the other person to show they like you first.
- Not making jokes, touching, or other overt displays of interest.
- Not investing extra attention into them.
- Not following up or asking out.
- Waiting until you're certain of acceptance before taking any pro-social risks.
- Waiting for them to kiss you first or make the first move.

These behaviors can be driven by various fears or self-protective beliefs—*it's uncool to show interest, it'll lead to overt rejection*, I'll appear weak, etc. No matter the cause, it's a big problem.

Hiding your interest prevents you from dating the people you like. Simple as that. These behaviors may feel safer in the short term, but in the long term they keep you from reaching your social and romantic goals. You can't get over dating anxiety without learning to show interest.

Trust me, I've been there too.

## How to End a Relationship Before it Starts

In college, I had psychology classes with a girl I really liked. She was smart and friendly. I met her the first night of my sophomore year. We had an immediate connection, so naturally I avoided her for another year. Luckily, after that year, we had more classes together. I eventually summoned the courage to invite her to my friend's house party one weekend. She said yes, and was clearly happy about it. Now, at the time—after a couple years of noticing that only the girls I didn't like seemed really into me—I was under the impression that showing interest would make her uninterested in me. I struggled with what to do. She was coming with me to the party, but I didn't want to kill the connection by seeming into her. My solution?

Well, I cringe even writing this down. She met me at my house, all smiley and dressed up, and we walked over to the party together, chatting along the way. When we got there, I introduced her to a couple of people, then I ignored her the rest of the night like a jerk. In a ham-fisted attempt to further our relationship, I pretended I didn't like her as much as I did, and I made a point of greeting, connecting with, and engaging as many other people at the party as possible. I checked in with her occasionally, and noticed she wasn't having a good time.

Towards the end of the night, she was sitting on the living room floor by herself looking miserable. This confused me because I thought I'd done a fairly good job: I didn't seem into her, and I showed her how cool I was by talking to a bunch of people. Surely that should have increased her attraction to me!

She let me walk her home, and I was very disappointed when she didn't want to go out with me again. I was so daft I even asked her friend what went wrong. I still feel bad about treating her that way, but it demonstrates the problem with being afraid to honestly communicate interest.

This issue actually resulted in me dating nobody for multiple years. I avoided people that I liked, many of whom actually appeared to be into me already. But I truly thought I had to hide my interest to keep their interest alive. It was a disastrous strategy. Time and time again, I watched initial interest flicker out and die. It was years before I challenged my underlying beliefs.

In hindsight, and with the wisdom of 20+ more years of experience, I see how naive my twisted assumptions really were. Of course, it wasn't my attraction itself that had caused my dating problems. It was how I responded to my attraction that drove people away.

## The Truth About the Friend Zone

Some people take this to an extreme and go out of their way to become "the nonsexual best friend." You invest heavily into a relationship without communicating your romantic intent. This leads to an inauthentic platonic relationship. Sometimes people refer to this as being in the "friend zone."

It's hard to get out of a friend zone situation because the dynamic of the relationship has already been established. It can feel like a big leap if you've been hiding your attraction, then you suddenly reveal it and catch the person off guard. It can feel like a bait and switch, which is painful for everybody involved.

Research into unrequited love finds that the longer you're friends with somebody, the less likely you are to date them. This is just one of the reasons why I encourage you to be honest and authentic upfront. If romantic feelings develop later in the relationship, then by all means explore them. But if you're entering a relationship under false pretenses, it's disrespectful, and it probably won't end well.

Unrequited love can really screw people up. I knew someone who didn't date for many, many years because she was holding out for one specific man...even after he got married and had a child.

I had a roommate in college who got caught in such an extreme case of unrequited love that it drove him practically crazy. He got so stuck in obsessively analyzing whether this one girl liked him that he stopped going to class or eating. He would corner people to have the same conversation again and again, presenting the evidence and trying to decipher whether she really liked him or not. His obsession became so bad that he actually dropped out of school. Unrequited love is one of the most painful dating experiences, and it does a lot of damage to your self-esteem.

People often enter the friend zone in part because they're not obvious enough about their true romantic interests, while those they're interested in are not clear enough about their lack of interest (often due to politeness). In the absence of clear communication, you're left to worry and ruminate on whether your crush likes you or not. Having seen the scenario play itself out, both in my life and in the lives of others, trust me: it's better to clearly show your interest. Telling the truth might cost you a cherished friendship or your fantasy of a potential relationship, but that's much better than maintaining a friendship that's built on a lie.

## HIDING YOUR INTEREST WASTES YOUR TIME

When a 31-year-old programmer came into treatment for dating anxiety, he reported having had a series of crushes on friends. Despite his natural charm, these crushes didn't turn into romantic relationships. He invested deeply in the women, cultivating what we referred to as "platonic girlfriends." While there were positive elements to these relationships, on the whole they were deeply unsatisfying to him because he actually wanted to date the women. He didn't take the risk to show his interest for fear that he would lose the not-entirely-unsatisfying connections he had. To him, these friendships were better than being alone.

Eventually, he noticed that these non-relationships lingered for a long time and they prevented him from pursuing real relationships. Before he knew it, the majority of his twenties had been squandered in this fashion. Much of our work was to help him become more overt with his interest. His honesty resulted in some of these women leaving his life. While he mourned the loss of these friends, he succeeded in developing other authentic and true romantic relationships.

## The Two Necessities to Build a Relationship

We are inclined to like people who like us. But this "reciprocity effect" is just the tip of the iceberg. We know from research that interpersonal attraction comes down to two factors, and you need both of them for attraction to occur: capacity and willingness.

### Capacity

Capacity is the arena where people spend their time and emotional energy, and where most of my patients believe they struggle. Capacity refers to all the traits someone uses to communicate their value to another person—the qualities in us that others value. When people talk about strengths or deficiencies in height, weight, muscularity, education, intelligence, or income, they're referring to capacity. The internet focuses on capacity, magazines focus on it, and when we talk to ourselves and explain our dating successes and failures, we most often chalk it up to capacity.

But your capacity differs depending on who's observing. What I consider to be an important trait is often very different from what somebody else believes. Capacity is about fit because value is in the eye of the beholder. Sure, certain traits like being tall and muscular might be more attractive to the average person, but that doesn't mean you can predict what any one individual considers most important (fortunately for me, being someone who is neither tall nor muscular).

There are only a few traits that almost all women and men want in a long-term partner. According to one 2007 chapter, those traits are: warmth and trustworthiness. How much time do you spend increasing your capacity with those? Probably not very much.

**A CHALLENGE FOR YOU**

I challenge you to test something: ask your friends what your appealing traits are. Try to get 25 and see how your perception of yourself changes.

## Willingness

As significant as capacity is, it doesn't lead to attraction without the second component: willingness. In the psychology field, willingness is deeply tied to trust: it's trust that the other person is motivated to act in your mutual benefit.

Willingness refers to the perception that you will share your positive qualities with another person. It's not just about being kind—it's about being kind to a specific person. In other words, how willing are you to invest in one person, or to treat that one person well, as opposed to someone else? Having highly valued traits or qualities is worthless to somebody if they believe that you won't invest time and energy in them as an individual.

Think about it: let's say you see an appealing celebrity eating at a restaurant. How much energy are you likely to spend courting them? Although their capacity is high (they have high social status, are popular, and good looking), you probably expect their willingness to be low (you assume they wouldn't be interested in an average person like you). Therefore, you don't pursue a relationship. In other words, no matter how appealing they are, you likely experience low interpersonal attraction towards them.

Someone's willingness is a fairly reliable way of figuring out if they're into you. Research has found that you can't guess from looking whether someone's into you. Instead, you have to rely on the time and energy they're willing to invest in you and the relationship. Investing in you, rather than the many other things they could be doing, is an honest and hard-to-fake indicator of their interest.

## YOUR BIGGER PROBLEMS ARE LIKELY WILLINGNESS, NOT CAPACITY

While your capacity will never be ideal, what is your willingness level?

- Are you warm to people you're into?
- Do you smile at them?
- Do you start conversations?
- Do you express interest and curiosity?
- Do you share about yourself, your emotions, your likes, and your opinions?
- Do you give attention when people you like are talking?
- Do you express your reactions to what they say?
- Do you try to bring good things into their lives?
- Do you invite them to activities?
- Do you organize get-togethers?
- Can everyone tell when you like somebody?

Many people are so focused on their perceived deficits in capacity, that they aren't aware of the importance of willingness. Sometimes people even mistakenly consider willingness to be *unattractive!* I had a friend growing up who was the embodiment of this. We used to go out to bars together, and he would grab his drink and pick somewhere to sit where he could focus on looking cool, detached, and like he was too good to be there. His willingness was so low that he barely deigned to talk to *me*. He would project high capacity, have some drinks, and then go home having talked to nobody.

High capacity + low willingness = no connection.

I have another friend who was the exact opposite. He gave very little thought to capacity, but was very high in warmth and willingness. His capacity was no higher than mine, but unlike me he spent no time obsessing over it. Also unlike me, he didn't think he had to feign disinterest. So he engaged, flirted, and joked with anybody he was drawn to. He was very successful in dating. In fact, he's one of the most socially successful people I've ever known.

Moderate capacity + high willingness
= many connections.

The good news is that while capacity is slow to change, we can change willingness in any given moment. Just by deciding to show interest, warmth, curiosity, and invest in someone else you can significantly increase your attractiveness. That change can potentially affect the trajectory of your dating life (remember those studies showing that far more men approached the moderately physically attractive but warm and smiling women at the bar?).

One of the best relationships in my twenties came about because of this. I made the choice to experiment being more obvious with my willingness and invested my time and interest in a kind, artistic, and rather shy woman. We dated for a while, and she actually told me later that she hadn't been immediately into me, but as I focused more time and attention on her (i.e., showed willingness) she became more interested in me.

## The Person You Like May Also Have Dating Anxiety

By showing your interest first, you can lower the other person's dating anxiety (remember, the majority of people report suppressing romantic interest out of fear). It's then easier for them to show their attraction because you've been a leader. People tend to reciprocate romantic interest—partly because it's exciting when we think someone likes us, but also because it makes it much safer to let interest and warmth flow. When you suppress your interest, you shut off the chance at connections before they get a chance to grow.

If you're reading this book, it's likely you're showing *even less* willingness than you realize. Based on what we've discussed, I'm sure you can see why it's so important to fix it.

## The One Step Willingness Test

Not sure whether you're obvious enough about your attraction? Here's a simple question you can ask yourself that will make it clear:

"When I like someone, can people tell?"

More often than not, the answer is no. The person you're attracted to doesn't know you like them, people around you don't know it, and maybe even your close friends can't tell. The more often you can change the answer to that question to "yes," the better dating success you'll have.

There's a good chance you're showing even less willingness than you realize. Especially when it matters.

## Invisible Overtures

I came across a study once that helped me put all this stuff into context. The study was called Invisible Overtures. The researchers sorted people into groups based on how much dating anxiety they had. Then they set up interactions with cross-sex partners. They engaged in person, and afterward the participants were asked two things:

*How attracted were you to your date?*

*How obvious and observable was your attraction?*

On the whole, the people felt their attraction was fairly obvious. But they were wrong. In fact, when the researchers asked interaction partners, they found the more the anxious people liked someone, the less obvious their attraction was. In other words, if an anxious person liked somebody, it appeared that they did not. They appeared more into people they didn't like. Just take a moment to consider all the ways that this would get in the way of a successful dating life.

The study was called Invisible Overtures because the participants believed they were showing clear signs of interest, when in fact they weren't. The researchers theorized that people often get what they feel is a lack of reciprocation, when in fact they appeared not to have shown any interest at all. To quote from the article: "Where [the participants] seem to err is in failing to appreciate how tentative and ambiguous those efforts [to signal attraction] appear to the object of their affection." The takeaway is that maybe you're not getting rejected—you just haven't been obvious enough in communicating your attraction.

This study made me think of an interaction I had in a sandwich shop with my friend. The girl behind the counter wasn't my type, but she seemed interested in me. This happened to me a lot at the time. I never got this reaction from women I liked—only women I wasn't interested in.

When I left the sandwich shop, I asked my friend about it. "Why do women I'm not into flirt with me?"

"It's because you're flirting with them!" he said indignantly. "You smile, make small talk, and joke around with them. You're friendlier with them than women you like."

"But I'm like that with everyone," I protested.

"No, you're not. You're so much friendlier to girls you don't like. You always do that. It's pretty funny actually."

I was only my friendly self around women I wasn't attracted to. From an outsider's perspective it was obvious, but I was so stuck in my head that I'd never noticed.

Like me, you probably have protective mechanisms that stop you from sending flirtatious signals, whether you realize it or not.

## Flirting Without Disaster:
## The Four Stages of Flirtation

I know the idea of being obvious with your interest feels scary, but our courtship rituals have built-in defenses for that fear: flirting.

Consider why people flirt: it allows us to show interest without being obvious or getting rejected. Flirtation gives you both plausible deniability. When you flirt, you hint at your attraction and see whether it's reciprocated before escalating to more obvious hints.

Based on extensive research, I use a model of flirtation broken down into a series of stages (based most strongly on an article by Egland and colleagues). I include it because a lot of people I work with don't know what showing interest looks like, so they don't know where to start. It's important to know this model so you can understand which stage of dating anxiety might be shutting you down, and where you could be more open.

### Stage 1: Politeness Flirtation

In this stage, you treat someone the way you'd treat any other person you aren't interested in. It's indistinguishable from politeness, where you're using the basic social skills you were taught as a kid: smile, make eye contact, ask questions, answer questions, and so on. In this stage, the name of the game is warmth, curiosity, and friendliness.

## Stage 2: Attentional Flirtation

In this stage, you continue to use good social skills, but you give the person you like extra attention and focus. Think of it as taking your core social skills and turning up the intensity. Smile at your crush more, make eye contact a little longer, ask more questions, and self-disclose more. This is beyond politeness—it's literally showing interest through attention. You want the other person thinking, "Are they flirting with me, or are they just a really friendly person?"

## Stage 3: Traditional Flirtation

This involves more overt and obvious indications of romantic interest. Things like teasing, push-pull, mixed signals, compliments, moving closer, and physical touch. The mix of signals means your intentions aren't completely overt, and you have some plausible deniability if they don't want to come along with you. You hope they think, "I'm pretty sure this person is into me, but I can't be certain."

## Stage 4: Overt Flirtation

Here your romantic interest becomes pretty clear. This is the stage where you verbally tell the other person you like them, ask them out, and make more unabashed indications of your attraction.

### STAGE 0 FLIRTING

I was in a social group with a girl I'd always liked, but I was intimidated by her. I finally interacted with her in a more authentic way that showed I liked her. She responded well, but told me she was confused. "I always thought you hated me!"

Even though I was always into her, I'd been so protected that I sent signals of disliking her. I wasn't even at stage 1 of flirting. I was at stage 0. I treated her with less than basic warmth and politeness—the way you'd treat someone you dislike. Essentially, it communicates rejection. I was an accidental master of stage 0.

Many of my patients fear that flirting or showing interest means leaping from having no interactions to stage 3. They worry everything they do will be weird and unexpected, which is exactly why we have stages 1 and 2. Luckily, in flirtation, the goal is not to jump right in. It's to slowly escalate.

## Showing Interest Lowers Anxiety

Counter-intuitively, using this flirtation model will reduce your dating anxiety. It's exposure therapy in action. This works in several distinct and powerful ways.

Firstly, as we focused on last chapter, safety behaviors contribute strongly to dating anxiety. By not showing interest, you prevent yourself from learning that doing so is safe. Look at some of those extraverted people who lack anxiety. They can flirt, show interest easily, and seem unperturbed when their reception is lukewarm. You can be like that too.

Allowing yourself to show your interest actually directly decreases your anxiety. It's surprising, but there are some fascinating reasons why.

Remember that social anxiety is a result of the gap between how you think you *should* behave and how you think you *are* behaving. For example, I was forever trying to come across as calm, cool, and disinterested in the women I liked. However, I was actually nervous and attracted (and desperately hoping they would like me). The gap between my performance demands and what I actually felt in the moment created anxiety. When I lowered my performance standards to naturally allow my romantic interest and authentic self to show, I erased the bulk of my anxiety.

Showing your interest in someone may be scary, but allowing yourself to do so freely will feel like unloading a great burden. But even if you still have anxiety when you like someone, it isn't a big deal. In fact, it can actually help you. As weird as it might seem, anxiety is an expected and powerful part of flirtation.

## Anxiety and Flirtation

Starting in the 1970s, brave researchers began entering bars with hidden cameras to identify how courtship actually worked in the real world. Anthropologist David Givens, Ph.D., observed that social anxiety was expected when strangers met, and found that many of our core signals during flirtation included displays of anxious physiological arousal (as well as signals for reassuring others). For example, the batting of eyelids is a combination of increased eye contact and the extra blinking that comes with anxiety. And you may recognize blushing as a symptom of anxious arousal, but it's also an attraction cue traditionally mimicked with makeup. Also, playing with our hair is a way of self-soothing when we're feeling anxious, as well as a way of attracting attention to a health signal.

So what mysterious factor transformed these otherwise anxious signals into flirtation signals? Warmth. Warmth + anxiety = flirtation. The anxiety shows that you're affected by the other person (you care how they respond), while the warmth shows your desire to connect (and that there's no reason for them to be afraid). This is why the myth of being cool and confident doesn't work: we're only cool and confident around strangers that don't matter to us. Conversely, being nervous around someone is a clear indicator that we're impacted by their presence, which shows we care about them.

### ANXIETY IS ATTRACTION

To take this idea one step further, in dating anxiety, what you think is fear might be better understood as attraction.

Consider your physiological responses to someone you like: your heart beats faster, you get butterflies in your stomach, you shake, etc. You might see them as only anxious responses, but aren't these the same sensations that signal romantic interest?

There's a reasonable chance you're simply interpreting your attraction as anxiety.

There's a very famous psychological study in which people were asked to cross one of two bridges over a ravine. Unbeknownst to the participants, there was an attractive person waiting for them on the other side. Once the participants crossed the bridge, that person on the other side was instructed to engage them in conversation. Here's the twist: two different bridges were used in the study. We'll call one the "experimental" bridge, and the other the "control" bridge. The experimental bridge was a five-foot wide, 450-foot long bridge made of wooden boards. It was attached to wire cables that ran from one side of a canyon to another.

The experimental bridge had many anxiety-inducing features: it had a tendency to wobble and sway, giving the impression that the participants might fall over the side; it had low handrails; and it hung precariously over a 230-foot drop to rocks and shallow rapids.

The control bridge was a solid wood bridge farther upriver. It was constructed of heavy cedar, and was much firmer and wider than the experimental bridge. It was only 10 feet high over a shallow rivulet, it had high handrails, and it did not sway at all.

The researchers discovered that people who met the person after crossing the experimental bridge were more sexual in their communication and more likely to attempt to get in contact with her afterwards. In other words, people were scared from crossing the bridge, but they interpreted their physiological responses (increased heart rate, shaking, sweating, etc.) as attraction. This study, and many others, show that our fear systems are not so different from our attraction systems. But importantly, this can go both ways: if you have significant dating anxiety, you might be interpreting your natural excitement and attraction as fear.

You might find that this overlap means you're able to reinterpret your physiological symptoms in a more effective way. One study showed that choosing to interpret your anxiety as excitement—simply telling yourself "I am excited"—lowers distress. Therefore, embrace your feelings of anxiety as strong indications that you find someone attractive. Then, instead of bottling those feelings up, show them naturally. If your hands shake, let them shake. If your heart pounds, let it pound. If you feel nervous, maybe say so. You'll be shocked at how much easier and more successful your dating life will be.

## Are You Afraid of Your Own Attraction?

When we say we have chemistry with another person, we're talking about a reaction. One person does something, the other person responds, and attraction occurs. Now, you can't force chemistry with another person. If they don't like you, they don't like you. But you have to at least give them the option. Any attraction that you hide, suppress, or protect against is an opportunity wasted, and a potential for love squandered.

Some people hide their attraction so well that they never date anyone they are truly into. For you, dating anxiety may be nothing more than the experience of an approach-avoidance conflict. One part of you wants to move toward something good, while another part of you wants to retreat from potential danger. Do yourself a favor. Reinterpret those feelings as attraction and excitement, and err on the side of approaching that feeling. The single most important factor in your dating life is the number of interactions you initiate. There's a strong and direct correlation between your dating effort and your dating success.

## Find Your Percentage

I want to hammer this point home: show your

attraction to the people you like because it helps you discover who's interested in you and who's not. Trying to analyze your interactions to figure out who likes you is a terrible trap (see: the earlier sections about the friend zone and unrequited love). Drop all of that. You have a different goal now. All you need to do is this: *show your interest to people you like and see if they reciprocate.*

Unbelievable though it may seem, there is a percentage of people who you would be attracted to, and who would be interested in you just as you are. If only they had a chance. Your goal is to find those people. Instead of trying to force someone who doesn't like you to like you, just show your authentic self and see if that person is in your unknown percentage of admirers.

If they aren't a good fit, that's perfect! Better to find out early than six months down the line.

## What If I'm not Good Enough to Date Yet?

You might be saying: "But my percentage is low right now. Shouldn't I focus on becoming more attractive before I seek a partner?" The answer is no, please don't. There is no greater or misguided justification for avoiding connection than trying to improve yourself first. Here's a secret: if you follow that path, you'll discover that you never feel good enough to start dating. I've seen it happen too many times: people put off dating indefinitely as they "improve" themselves. Then, months or years later, they're still alone, except now they're mad at themselves for their lack of progress. This becomes a new reason not to initiate any dating effort. It's a sad cycle. Even if you get in great shape, for example, your anxiety will switch to your next perceived deficiency. Don't fall into this trap. You're good enough to date exactly as you are in this moment.

If you see someone who might fit in your percentage, talk to them. Show your attraction by flirting, and see if it's reciprocated. There isn't much to lose—you're just seeing whether they're part of your percentage. You're not converting anyone, just moving their category from unknown to known. And remember: the flirtation process is there to protect you if you feel anxious. If they are not interested, go ahead and feel disappointed, but be proud of yourself for taking the risk.

## No More Catastrophizing, No More Mindreading

Two of the biggest thinking problems you can experience with dating anxiety are:

- Catastrophizing about how bad everything will be
- Imagining that you can mindread

Your days of mindreading are over. You are no longer responsible for figuring out whether someone is into you. Instead, just show your interest (using the flirting scale and seeing if they reciprocate and invest in you). Do this, and people will quickly sort themselves into your percentage or out of it. And they will do so, as we will discuss in the next chapter, in surprisingly empathetic and polite ways.

Trying to get people who don't like you to like you takes a lot of (usually wasted) effort. I know the idea is seductive, but it's statistically a waste of time. Once you stop trying to force people into your percentage, and instead treat flirting as a discovery process, life gets a lot easier.

## Attraction Is a Great Thing

Your dating experiences will improve greatly once you stop trying to protect yourself against your own attraction. Feel your attraction fully. Then allow yourself to express it naturally and nonverbally.

Make it your goal to project your attraction outwards, so people around you can tell when you like someone. Making your attraction more obvious is a far more powerful improvement than lifting weights, reading self-help books, becoming funnier, and making more friends *combined*.

That's what my patient from the beginning of the chapter discovered. He was so used to hiding his attraction, that he almost never talked to girls he was interested in.

After we worked on showing his attraction, he completely transformed. At one point in treatment he attended a comic book convention. It was one of those conventions where people dress up like their favorite sci-fi characters. He talked to a lot of women he found attractive there. He took the risk of giving more attention to people he liked, and he quickly found women in his percentage (who liked him and he liked back). While some women at the convention were polite but non-responsive, a decent amount flirted back. However, he still struggled to ask them out.

We then did experiments to test an insidious assumption of his: that if you asked a woman for her phone number or asked her explicitly on a date, she would be offended that you assumed romantic interest. To his surprise, when we tested this assumption, he discovered that everyone responded positively, even if they weren't interested.

Half of the women never texted him back, and that was great news—because it meant half of them did. Soon he found himself going on a series of dates, and again he had to work on the next level of anxiety (flirting, kissing, etc.). Each step of the way, his dating anxiety wanted him to pull back, protect himself, hide his interest, and wait for the other person to make the moves.

Instead, he took the risk of being more authentic, and he overcame much of his dating anxiety. As a result, he's built a fulfilling social life and he's had a series of relationships.

But, in the process, he had to face many experiences where people did not reciprocate his interest. That's right, we need to talk about the dark beating heart of dating anxiety: it's time to overcome your fear of rejection.

# Show Your Interest

People need to know that you like them since
it's a major driver of falling in love

Aron, A., Dutton, D. G., Aron, E. N., & Iverson, A. (1989).
Experiences of falling in love. *Journal of Social and
Personal Relationships, 6*(3), 243–257.

Aron, A., Aron, E. N., & Allen, J. (1998). Motivations for
unreciprocated love. *Personality and Social Psychology
Bulletin, 24*(8), 787-796.

## The Truth About the Friend Zone

Your friend doesn't want to date you

Afifi, W. A., & Faulkner, S. L. (2000). On being 'just friends':
The frequency and impact of sexual activity in cross-sex
friendships. *Journal of Social and Personal Relationships,
17*(2), 205–222.

Reeder, H. M. (2000). "I like you…as a friend": The role of
attraction in cross-sex friendship. *Journal of Social and
Personal Relationships, 17*(3), 329–348.

Lack of clear communication leads to unrequited love

Baumeister, R. F., Wotman, S. R., & Stillwell, A. M. (1993).
Unrequited love: On heartbreak, anger, guilt, scriptlessness,
and humiliation. *Journal of Personality and Social
Psychology, 64*(3), 377–394.

## The Two Necessities to Build a Relationship

We like people who like us

Greitemeyer, T. (2010). Effects of reciprocity on attraction:
The role of a partner's physical attractiveness. *Personal
Relationships, 17*(2), 317-330.

When we think others like us, we act
in ways that make it happen

Curtis, R. C., & Miller, K. (1986). Believing another likes or
dislikes you: Behaviors making the beliefs come true.
*Journal of Personality and Social Psychology, 51*(2), 284–
290.

Two factor model of attraction: capacity and willingness

Penke, L., Todd, P. M., Lenton, A. P., & Fasolo, B. (2007). How
self-assessments can guide human mating decisions.
In G. Geher & G. Miller (Eds.), *Mating intelligence: Sex,
relationships, and the mind's reproductive system* (pp.
37–75). Lawrence Erlbaum Associates Publishers.

Montoya, R. M., & Horton, R. S. (2014). A two-dimensional
model for the study of interpersonal attraction. *Personality
and Social Psychology Review, 18*(1), 59–86.

Boothby, E. J., & Bohns, V. K. (2021). Why a simple act of
kindness is not as simple as it seems: Underestimating the
positive impact of our compliments on others. *Personality &
social psychology bulletin, 47*(5), 826–840.

It's hard to tell from looking if someone finds you attractive

Place, S. S., Todd, P. M., Penke, L., & Asendorpf, J. B. (2009).
The ability to judge the romantic interest of others.
*Psychological Science, 20*(1), 22–26.

Grammer, K., Kruck, K., Juette, A., & Fink, B. (2000). Nonverbal behavior as courtship signals: The role of control
and choice in selecting partners. *Evolution and Human
Behavior, 21*(6), 371–390.

Hall, J. A., Xing, C., & Brooks, S. (2015). Accurately detecting
flirting: Error management theory, the traditional sexual
script, and flirting base rate. *Communication Research,
42*(7), 939–958.

Kerr, L.G., Borenstein-Laurie, J., & Human, L.J. (2020). Are
some first dates easier to read than others? The role of
target well-being in distinctively accurate first impressions.
*Journal of Research in Personality, 88*(1), 1-8.

## Invisible Overtures

Our romantic interest may not be as obvious as we think

Vorauer, J. D., Cameron, J. J., Holmes, J. G., & Pearce, D. G. (2003). Invisible overtures: Fears of rejection and the signal amplification bias. *Journal of Personality and Social Psychology, 84*(4), 793.

Montoya, R. M., & Sloat, N. T. (2019). People do not always act as positively as they feel: Evidence of affiliation suppression. *International Review of Social Psychology, 32*(1), Article 9

## Flirting Without Disaster: The Four Stages of Flirtation

Flirting is plausible deniability

Gecas, V., & Libby, R. (1976). Sexual behavior as symbolic interaction. *Journal of Sex Research, 12*(1), 33–49.

The four stages of flirtation

Egland, K. L., Spitzberg, B. H., & Zormeier, M. M. (1996). Flirtation and conversational competence in cross-sex platonic and romantic relationships. *Communication Reports, 9*(2), 105-117.

## Anxiety and Flirtation

Flirtation includes signals of anxious arousal

Givens, D. B. (2006). Love signals: A practical field guide to the body language of courtship. New York: Griffin.

Misinterpreting other experiences as anxiety

Dutton, D. G., & Aron, A. P. (1974). Some evidence for heightened sexual attraction under conditions of high anxiety. *Journal of Personality and Social Psychology, 30*(4), 510–517.

Alden, L., & Bieling, P. (1998). Interpersonal consequences of the pursuit of safety. *Behaviour Research and Therapy, 36*(1), 53-64.

Savitsky, K., & Gilovich, T. (2003). The illusion of transparency and the alleviation of speech anxiety. *Journal of Experimental Social Psychology, 39*(6), 618-625.

Reinterpreting anxiety as excitement
Brooks A. W. (2014). Get excited: Reappraising pre-performance anxiety as excitement. *Journal of Experimental Psychology. General, 143*(3), 1144–1158.

# CHAPTER 8

. . .

# Overcoming the Fear of Rejection

Way back in the beginning of the book I told you about my rejection month in grad school, when I had to ask out the stranger I found most attractive each day for 30 days. It was as horrifying as it sounds. By day 30, I could laugh off a rejection pretty easily. But rejection month didn't start that way. As you can imagine, day one was by far the worst.

I panicked every time I saw a young woman that first day in Harvard Square. My heart was pounding, I couldn't breathe, and I was shaking so badly I could barely walk. I psyched myself out, over and over again—I'd see a girl, try to walk towards her, then slink into the nearby 7-Eleven to hide. I did that for three hours before I realized I couldn't repeat this pattern forever. I had to do something.

So I walked out of the 7-Eleven and saw a girl sitting near the subway station entrance. She was the one. As I walked her way, I was terrified her protective boyfriend would pop out of a nearby alleyway and attack me. Every cell in my body screamed at me to run away, even as she sat there innocently playing on her phone.

Finally I was in front of her, my voice shaking uncontrollably. "Um, hi."

She looked at me and said something I can't remember. I was panicking so much I'm surprised I can remember any of it at all. She was polite, but clearly uninterested. I walked away feeling like a piece of absolute crap. I couldn't believe how foolish I'd been to think she'd want some dork like me to ruin her day. Who was I to make her feel uncomfortable like that? Why did I choose to override my gut reaction to run away before I had the chance to embarrass myself?

I wondered why the hell I'd chosen to do this. Maybe my protection system was on to something. I couldn't imagine a woman finding me attractive ever again. And yet, I was about to wake up and do it again the next day...

Until now, I haven't told many people about rejection month (for various reasons we'll get into later). But I'm about to tell you about it here because this topic is so important. Much of the book so far has been based on my patients' experiences, experiments I've done, and extensive research. In the process of learning everything in the book up to this point:

- I'd stripped away the protective armor that prevented my connections with people.
- I started to show more of the real me and found true acceptance.
- I purposely projected my attraction to women I liked.
- I got more reciprocation for my attention.
- Everything generally went better for me in my dating life.

I know that for a lot of people, this would've been enough. But I wasn't content with doing fine. Dating anxiety was an important issue for me, and I wanted to help others. I knew I wouldn't be happy with myself unless I stood up to my deepest social anxiety. I had to face my fear of rejection.

That's when I learned about exposure therapy in grad school. As a refresher: the idea behind exposure therapy is that if you face your fears rather than avoid them, you can get used to them, become realistic about the level of danger, habituate, and no longer be afraid of them. I wondered if I could use this process to overcome my fear of rejection.

I imagined what life might look like if I was no longer afraid of rejection. I'd be able to talk to anybody, no matter how intimidating I found them. I could truly be myself, even if I was talking to a stranger. This was the promise of exposure therapy.

Shortly after I discovered exposure therapy, I was talking with a friend about his dating issues at a late-night diner. I asked him, "Would you be willing to face a string of overt, true rejections from women, if it meant you'd be able to find the girl of your dreams?"

He thought for a moment as he chewed, then said, "Hell no."

And that may be your answer, too. But for me, the answer was a resounding 100% yes. So rejection month was born.

I'll be perfectly frank: this is a scary chapter. Even as I look back on that time in my life, it's still a little scary to write about. Everything we've discussed so far has been your anxiety's complex attempts to protect you from one thing: rejection. And we're going to face it directly in this chapter.

If dating anxiety were a video game, this would be the final boss at the end. This is the true nemesis you must overcome to get the treasure you desire. The bad news is that you have to go through this to get the connection you want. The good news is that you *can* go through it.

In this chapter, you'll learn the truth about rejection in dating experiences. While it's painful, the consequences are internal and emotional, with little to no real-world impact. You'll learn that rejection is surprisingly polite, you can cope when it inevitably happens, and it's possible to get so used to it that it hardly affects you at all.

And the secret is in exposure therapy.

## How Exposure Therapy Works

There are two ways to do exposure therapy: graduated exposure and flooding.

Graduated exposure means you work your way from your smallest fear to your greatest fear in small steps. You only escalate to more difficult fears when you become comfortable with your current fear. This is the humane approach to exposure therapy, the one I recommend for you, and the one that I use with patients.

During my rejection month, though, I took the other approach: flooding. This is where you flood yourself with the most anxious situation from the very beginning. If you're afraid of heights, you go straight to the top of the Empire State Building. If you're afraid of spiders, you let tarantulas crawl over you for four hours. And if you're me and you're afraid of rejection, you talk to the most intimidating woman you see each day and ask her out. It's a painful form of exposure therapy.

Painful, but effective.

I was leading a dating group recently, and one of the members talked to me after the session. "How do you avoid getting rejected?" he asked. He seemed pretty concerned about it.

"Well, tell me what usually happens. What typical circumstances usually lead up to your rejections?" I thought he might mention some common problems like not flirting, making big leaps instead of slow progression, or picking the wrong people.

"Oh, I've never been rejected," he said.

I smiled and told him his question should've been, "How can I get more *experience* with rejection?"

I find that the people who have the least experience with rejection tend to be most afraid of it, due to lack of familiarity or exposure. What he was really asking was, "How can I succeed and meet my goals without learning to deal with rejection, failure, or disappointment?"

Who wouldn't want that? I can't tell you how many times I've given up pursuing what I wanted just to avoid the possibility of rejection. But our goal shouldn't be to avoid rejection. Instead we should learn how to handle it, take away its power, and move forward toward our goals anyway.

After all, those who succeed tend to be familiar with rejection and failure.

I have a friend who started four companies that went out of business. Then he hit it big on the fifth, and *really* big on the sixth. Do you think anyone cares about the failures that preceded his success? Absolutely not.

Michael Jordan is one of the most successful basketball players of all time, yet here's what he once said about failure:

"I've missed more than 9,000 shots in my career. I've lost almost 300 games. Twenty-six times, I've been trusted to take the game-winning shot and missed. I've failed over and over and over again in my life. And that is why I succeed."

I talked to my mother about this once. She's a classically trained actress from Scotland, and she told me about her experience auditioning for roles. She went through a series of almost guaranteed rejections. It sounded terrible.

> Mark Ruffalo's first audition was to be a turtle at Busch Gardens and he didn't get it. Then he was rejected 600 more times before getting his first acting job.

My mother said that once you've done enough auditions, you don't really get nervous anymore, and you no longer feel rejected or full of shame afterward. It just feels like part of the process. This is exposure therapy in action. You have to face your failure enough times to teach your emotional brain that it's okay. But if you don't face that rejection enough, it will own you. In fact, in acting school my mum knew some amazing actors, but many of them couldn't handle the pain of audition rejections, so they gave up acting entirely after school.

## The Pain of Rejection and the Downward Spiral

Why are we so afraid of rejection?

In short, because it's terrifying and it sucks. We're built to suffer when we're rejected. In the immediate aftermath of a rejection, we suffer two experiences. Firstly, we have a self-esteem drop. We feel like we've just discovered we weren't as valuable as we thought we were. We feel bad about ourselves, then we start to assume other people must agree, and that everyone we know sees us as less valuable than we believed. We even feel like our friends like us less after we've experienced a rejection.

Secondly, we experience actual pain. The social pain of rejection lights up your brain as though you're in physical pain. That's why people describe rejection with words like agony and suffering. No wonder we want to avoid it.

It doesn't matter who we are or who's reject- ing us: unless we do exposure therapy to reset our system, we feel pain from rejection no matter what. I discovered one striking study that taught me this. The study tracked emotional distress responses in participants as they played an online game of ball toss with people (they believed to be) from different groups—everyone from the KKK to democrats.

When the participants were instructed to play with the KKK group, they were rejected - no one threw them the virtual ball. The study found that the participants, who were decent people who wanted nothing to do with the KKK, still felt the pain of rejection when the KKK excluded them. In other words, even if you hate a group of people, you can still suffer when they reject you.

Patients sometimes say to me, "I barely even liked that person, why am I so bothered by their rejection?" That's how we're built. Rejection is such a powerful response it *doesn't even matter if you know the rejection is fake*. People in one study were told in advance that a computer simulation was going to be ostracizing them in a virtual group, and there were no other humans involved, yet they still had the same emotional rejection experience.

We are built to suffer in the face of rejection.

Unfortunately, the news gets worse. The real problem with rejection is not this short-term discomfort, but the long-term effects. It's something I came to know as "the downward spiral." The downward spiral is the idea that the more you get rejected, the more rejectable you become. Have you noticed that after you suffer a social injury, you're not warm, friendly, and at your social best? In fact, you're in a bad mood and you want to go home, even if there are other social opportunities in front of you.

Now imagine you suffer a whole bunch of rejections in a row. What might that do to you? A lot of studies have shown that one rejection makes the next one more likely. After a rejection we think and behave differently: often we become less helpful, we start acting mean, we're more likely to punish people, we act cold, and we assume the worst about people. Not the kind of behavior that'll win you many dates, is it?

Other research reveals that lonely people are plagued with a special way of thinking. Lonely people feel dismissed and unwanted in situations where others feel welcomed. And so continues the downward spiral.

Why are we built this way? At its core, your dramatic response to rejection is preventing you from doing something dangerous again. It hits you with shame, guilt, disgust, and every other weapon at its disposal to get you to play it safe. When someone you're interested in rejects you, your brain tells you to stay in your place, get the hell away from others, and lick your wounds in the corner of the cave where you can't bother anybody. Your brain says, "Don't you dare try talking to someone you're attracted to again. You aren't good enough for any of them." Again—scary stuff.

Are you feeling terrified yet and vowing to never leave your room? Well, I certainly was. I knew all about rejection research and the dreaded downward spiral before I started rejection month. I hoped I could experience enough rejections that I would eventually be unmoved by them.

But what if I went into a downward spiral instead?

What if I experienced so many rejections that I became cold, bitter, and isolated? What if I ruined my social life and plummeted into depression? These were serious questions and serious risks. I thought about it for a long time before moving forward. But I knew I had to respect the downward spiral, and set up rejection month so I could cope with the pain.

## Most Rejections Are Polite

Secretly, I hoped that I'd never have to actually face rejection. I would start talking to women I liked and realize that everything was just fine and none of them would reject me. Although I told myself my goal was to face rejection, maybe I wouldn't have to.

The good news is that my avoidant wishes didn't come true. I was continually, uniformly, emphatically, and deeply rejected for a whole month. And yes, this was good news. Because I was able to face my deepest fear, take a good look at it, get to know it, and in doing so it became less scary. Every day, without a break, I went up to a stranger I was attracted to, communicated interest, and got shut down. A striking 0% of these interactions turned into dates. And it was a great victory.

Despite not yielding any dates, rejection month was one of the most powerful experiences of my life. When I imagined rejection, I pictured those terrible scenes in teen movies. The nerdy guy talks to the popular girl. She looks disgusted, then she sneers some insults along the lines of, "As if someone like me would talk to somebody like you," thus crushing his self-worth. It's harsh, it's public, and, most importantly, it's fiction.

What I encountered during rejection month was very different. Here's a brief list of some things I experienced:

- Women said "no" to me, but very few people actually *rejected* me. Everybody was kind, thoughtful, and put effort into managing my feelings and saving face for me.

- Multiple women told me they'd like to meet up for a date, but they were about to leave the country.
- Some women gave me their phone numbers, but never responded when I texted (this is a form of delayed rejection that people use to be polite).
- I met a lot of women who said they had boyfriends. Of course, I have no idea how many of them *actually* had boyfriends.

The point is: people were strikingly polite with their rejections. The most common way people show a lack of interest on a first meeting is by simply being less encouraging. They're usually not derisive or dismissive, and they don't signal disgust. Instead, they'll give short responses to questions, won't ask many questions of their own, remain disconnected, and find polite ways to leave the conversation.

**CAN YOU READ THE SIGNS?**

If you have a hard time gauging whether people are into you, that's great news—it's because people are

> *too* nice. Studies show that it's hard to tell who's attracted to you and who's not because strangers who aren't into us still tend to be warm, friendly, and polite.
>
> Now, let's say you're on a date. Those same studies show that most people are soft and non-confrontational when they signal their disinterest on a date. They do things like create more physical space or invest less in the conversation. In other words, they "reject" by simply not being encouraging.

The vast majority of people want to be nice, even if they're rejecting you. One 2010 study backed up this assertion. Alan Goodboy and Maria Brann, the researchers, studied the behaviors of 21 college students to study how people prefer to end unwanted advances. They discovered five different behaviors people use to reject flirtation. Consider if any of them seem familiar:

1. Departure (leaving the situation)
2. Friendship networks (friends step in to distract and eject)
3. Cell phone usage (pretending to receive a call or text)
4. Ignoring (not responding flirtatiously or turning away)
5. Facial expressions (dirty looks, lack of eye contact, etc.)

What initially struck me about these methods of rejection was their banality. They're generally innocuous. Sure, they're not all super nice, but none of them resemble the fever dream rejections we often imagine. Importantly, according to the study, the most common form of rejection is departure. Not humiliation, not shaming, not disgusted looks, just the simple act of getting out of the situation.

One participant in the study put it perfectly: "I definitely think leaving is always the best thing to do. You can do it in a nice way." That's how most people want to reject someone they're not drawn to: in the nicest, least confrontational way possible.

For the most part, people want to keep their rejections polite at every stage of dating. For example, a 1987 study by the popular old school dating researchers Perper and Weis tested how women tend to reject men on a second date. The most common strategies the women reported were:

- Avoiding acting in a way that was encouraging (like not touching him)
- Avoiding intimate situations (like finding excuses not to end up alone)
- Ignoring his flirtation attempts (sound familiar?)

- Focusing the conversation on unromantic topics and activities ("Did I tell you about my dad's weird skin problem?")

Once again, the most popular rejection strategies are nice, nonconfrontational, and allow you to save face. Most rejections weren't even rejections—they're just a lack of encouraging behaviors. Most people will actively go out of their way to minimize hurting your feelings. In fact, most research on unrequited love suggests that's why some men pine after women who aren't interested in them: because women's rejections are so sweet and subtle that the men don't take the hint.

Hopefully the message is clear at this point. But if it isn't, here's the fact: when people reject someone, they do it nicely. In fact, it's so nice that we could stop calling it "rejection" and instead call it an "absence of attraction" and it'd be just as accurate.

Yes, there are exceptions—some people are mean when they communicate disinterest. We've all had that happen. But they are the exceptions that prove the rule: they stand out precisely because they're so rare.

Now is a good time to point something out. You absolutely should be rejected if you overstep someone's boundaries. If you persist when somebody says no or you ignore someone's feelings, then you're likely to get a harsher rejection. As you should.

## The Internal Effects of Rejection

This is all well and good, but you're still thinking, "I don't care how polite a rejection is. It still hurts." You're absolutely right: rejection is painful, and even polite rejection can create a downward spiral. I felt that firsthand as my rejection month progressed.

After the first few rejections, I felt disappointed, creepy, and down in the dumps immediately afterward. Luckily, those feelings lifted pretty quickly each day. Then things got scary. After a week of very polite rejections, I could feel the pull of a downward spiral starting inside me. I felt I was disgusting, and I wanted to stay away from people so I wouldn't bother them. If I had given in to the downward spiral, I would have really been in trouble. I would have avoided social interactions altogether, which would deprive me of any positive social feedback. All of a sudden, my social circle would shrink because I was at home so much. In isolation, I would have further evidence that nobody liked me, which reinforces the perception that I'm disgusting, and that I was a bad person for making people feel uncomfortable by bothering them with my unwanted advances. If I didn't have my rules in place, I would have stayed in my room and never talked to another woman again. Luckily, no matter how low I got, I always asked out one woman each day and sought support from my friends and psychologist.

See, the dangers of rejection are not in the external world. They're internal, they're emotional, and they're frightening. I want to be clear: I do not recommend doing a rejection month. What I went through is part of the reason I recommend *graduated* exposure rather than flooding exposure therapy. It's really hard to absorb repeated rejections without it negatively affecting how you think about yourself, other people, and the future. Work your way through it with resilience and tons of support.

## Coping with Rejection

My hypothesis on this matter is controversial, so be warned: I believe the downward spiral of emotion I experienced in rejection month wasn't even the problem. The problem was that it compels us to stop engaging socially. In the end, this realization is why I escaped: I had rules in place that kept me going out there and interacting with people, despite rejections.

The less you engage with people *after* you're rejected, the more negatively you'll think about yourself and others. In isolation, you'll spiral downwards. Instead, recognize your feelings as a natural response, then use your friends to help you move forward (more on that in a moment). If I had given into the downward spiral during rejection month, I would have been in a much worse place emotionally than when I started. I would've ruminated on my failures, thought worse of myself, and probably continued to avoid people.

Most people who give dating advice don't put enough thought into the pain of rejection. Even fewer respect the power of multiple rejections. People tell you to buck up and move to the next one. But we know the emotional pain of rejection is real. You will feel that pain, and a few platitudes won't talk you out of it. Instead, what you can do is actively cope with it.

In fact, I tell this to almost all of my patients: take all the energy you'd normally put into avoiding rejection and instead direct it to meeting as many people as possible and setting up methods of recovering emotionally after the inevitable rejections.

The single most effective rejection coping method is social support. Positive relationships make it possible to tolerate social injury. A 1987 study tested people's response to failure in light of their relationships. Participants who thought about a warm, supportive person before failing at a task were more likely to attribute their failure to situational factors rather than personal outcomes. Conversely, participants who thought about a critical person before failing a task were more likely to exhibit shame-like responses, and attribute their failure to broad negative conclusions about their personality.

My conclusion from this study, and many others, is that you need people to support you to help you out of low places (e.g., romantic rejection). There are two main types of support:

- **Instrumental Support**—when someone helps you set goals and take the necessary steps to succeed.
- **Emotional Support**—someone you can communicate with about the experience you're going through. They will encourage you, too.

It's great to have people to talk to when you get rejected, or when you feel like you're not good enough. One theory is that the pain of rejection is caused by a temporary lapse in your need for belonging. So a good way to cope with rejection is to find belonging in others, or even remind yourself of your current connections. This can be in the form of spending time with your friends, remembering times you were accepted, and looking at photos that make you happy. Before I started the rejection month I had a large support structure deliberately in place, including professionals and my closest confidants, for this very reason.

But coping is more than just support. You also need to work on tolerating your painful thoughts and feelings. This means getting to a place where you can experience negative emotions without getting lost in them. Meditation and mindfulness techniques can be useful here, as well as responding to the painful thoughts and feelings with curiosity.

If left to their own devices, emotions usually rise and fall over a short period of time, rather than lasting forever like we fear. When you feel the pain of rejection, ask yourself:

"How long will it take for this emotion to drop by half?"

I practice this with many of my patients. One guy thought if he was rejected, he'd be distraught for a week or more. He also thought he'd never be able to talk to another woman again. But when we actually faced his pain after a rejection head on, he discovered that the intense pain only lasted for about an hour. By the next day, it was gone completely. He noted that something so temporary probably wasn't worth running away from forever.

The point is: you can't completely prevent the pain of rejection. But you can choose to press on no matter what you think or feel. Ask yourself, "Is it *physically* possible to say hello to a person even if I feel negative feelings and think negative thoughts?"

The answer is yes. So press on. The downward spiral's greatest power is in its ability to convince you to hide in seclusion.

**THE COALITION OF SINGLE WOMEN**

One rejection does not predict whether the next person you talk to will be interested in you. It makes me think of an old Onion article with a title like: "The Coalition of Single Women Votes No on Mitch." That article is making a joke of a common thought process: that one rejection means something is inherently wrong with you, everyone agrees there's something wrong with you, and everyone will always find something wrong

with you. These attributions lead people to feel depressed and lonely. Someone not being interested is
not a referendum on you. A rejection is just a lack of
fit for one person, not all people.

## Habituating to Rejection

So what happens when you persist through the
valley of the downward spiral and keep experiencing rejections? Well, I can't speak for everyone— but
I can tell you what happened to me.

Psychologically, I was in a bad state after a few
weeks. I felt worthless, romantically hopeless, and
I believed no woman would find me attractive ever
again because I was a piece of crap. Thank god I had
friends to support me. I had no interest or motivation to continue, but I persisted because I had a plan
in place and I'd promised myself that I'd reach my
goal. I was still suffering every day when it came
time for me to get rejected. But the rejections themselves started to matter less. There was no longer a
great crash, no drop in self-esteem, no more pain
than I was already experiencing. *Another rejection?
Fine, throw it on the pile with all the others.* This shift
was the start of a great change that was to follow.

Getting rejected just became part of my day that
I had to get through. As the rejections started to
bother me less, I also noticed that my anxiety was

dropping. I no longer paced around trying to work up the courage to say "hi" to somebody. I would just see somebody, know it was time, and walk up to talk to them. I would complete my rejection and move on. The exposure process was actually working.

## Ending Your Abusive Relationship with Anxiety

There's an unexpected pride that comes with doing exposure therapy. People don't talk about it much, and it's not emphasized in the research, but it's one of the most powerful effects that I notice in treatment. I think this positive feeling is a result of no longer being dominated by our own anxiety.

Psychologically, our anxiety bosses us around and stops us from doing things we want to do. It's a truly abusive relationship. We give up potential relationships—the most important part of our lives— because the anxiety has power over us. But when you start doing exposure therapy, you change that relationship. You're no longer submissive to your fears. Instead, you're like the kid who stands up to his bully in the movies. Sometimes, the bully only picks on you because they assume you won't fight back. But once you confront your bully, they may hit you hard, and it might hurt, but you realize something: you survived. No matter the outcome, you'll be very proud of yourself.

One of my clients excitedly told me a story about asking out his crush. "She said no, because she has a boyfriend," he said with a big smile. His joy wasn't based on the outcome at all. He was proud because he'd finally turned the tables on his anxiety and refused to be dominated.

That's how I felt during rejection month. After several weeks of relentless rejections, I started to feel my self-esteem creep back up. And this wasn't because people were suddenly into me—they most certainly were not—but I was into me. I was doing something I'd always wanted to do, but was too scared to try.

I used to tell people that the worst part of dating anxiety was when I wanted to talk to somebody, but I was too scared to do it. So I went home full of regret at what might have been. This is backed up by a lot of research: you suffer more because of your missed opportunities than your rejections. I can't be the only person who sits around with friends talking about that girl at the bar who was so obviously into me, but I missed all the signs or failed to take action in the moment.

That didn't happen anymore. I was becoming the person I'd always wanted to be. Or, more accurately, I was *allowing* myself to be the person I'd always been.

Strangely, the fact that the women I talked to weren't into me mattered less as the month went on. I was becoming too self-confident to care.

## The True Meaning of Self-Confidence

People often think self-confidence comes from the belief that you are great, valuable, high-status, and admired by others. Based on that belief, you try to appear self-confident by puffing yourself out, looking tough, or (worst of all) acting "dominant." But let's look more deeply at the phrase *self-confident* for a clue to what it really means.

Fident comes from the Latin word *fidelis* meaning faithful. Add *con*, meaning with, then *self*, and you get a distinct picture of true self-confidence: it means faithfulness to yourself. In other words, self-confidence means saying what you think, showing who you truly are, and being faithful to your beliefs. Enacting this version of self-confidence can be a lot quieter and subtler than posturing to dominate people. But it's also more powerful...

## Rejection Exposure in the Real World

Do I really want you to go out and torture yourself with your own form of flooding exposure therapy like rejection month?

Please don't.

Seriously, *please don't.*

Graduated exposure is the humane way of doing exposure therapy. You slowly work your way up the ladder from easy exposures to scary ones. If you've been taking more risks as you've read this book, maybe you've already started graduated exposure. Take all the things you're afraid of doing or you've been avoiding, write them down, then arrange them in order from easiest to hardest—there, you've got an anxiety hierarchy. Start from the easiest, desensitize yourself one item at a time, and work your way up the hierarchy.

Here's an example of an anxiety hierarchy, from easiest to hardest:

- Making eye contact with a someone you find attractive.
- Smiling at someone you find attractive.
- Saying hello to a random stranger.
- Saying hello to a stranger that you find appealing.

- Having a conversation with someone you find attractive.
- Asking someone you like on a date.

When I did rejection month, I deliberately went for the scariest item on my list, asking out a stranger I found attractive, and experienced it over and over again in a short period of time. Again, this is called flooding and I don't recommend you do this. It was helpful, but it's not what I do with my clients. In fact, I don't even ask people to seek out rejection deliberately. Instead, I encourage people to move pro-socially towards what you want—initiating conversations, being polite, flirting, showing interest, investing in relationships, asking people out—and work with the rejections that organically come up. These will occur, and they will be smaller and more natural.

And when you do discover there's no fit with a particular person (rejection), you get to practice your emotional regulation skills. This is really important and helpful, because if you know you can emotionally handle rejection, you don't need to be afraid of being warm, friendly, and taking pro-social risks to connect. You can step back, name your feeling (pain, shame, anger, a self-esteem drop, a desire to hide), then choose what you'll do to take care of yourself.

Post-rejection is a time for self-compassion. Some good methods for dealing with your rejection include:

- Seek out your friends for listening and emotional support, advice, encouragement, or just to have fun and get your mind off things.
- Supplement with "social snacking and shielding." This means you meet your needs for connection through memories, photos of friends, mood-congruent music, and self-affirmation.
- Engage in some expressive writing to look your negative thoughts in the face.
- Don't dedicate time to wallow in sad passivity—this will make things worse.
- Notice the physical sensations you experience with your emotions, and watch them shift. Getting out of your head and into your body can be very useful in allowing your feelings to pass through.
- Meditate.
- Exercise. You get clear benefits within about 20 minutes of physical exertion, and it has great side effects.

- Write a pride diary as you move towards your goals. Exposure is hard, so support yourself by highlighting the progress you're making every time you do something your anxiety wants you to avoid. Write, "I'm proud of myself because today I..." and fill in your exposures (or other exercises from this book). Encourage yourself like you would if you were a child working on something really difficult. I did this every day for a year at one point and it made a huge impact on my self-esteem.

- Finally, and most importantly, keep moving forward towards your goals. I can't tell you how many times a patient got rejected, only to have a great reaction from someone else shortly afterwards. Continuing to pursue your goals prevents you from generalizing broadly from a single rejection, and getting caught in the riptide. Remember, the downward spiral wants you to stop moving forward.

## THE GOOD FIT FALLACY

Imagine you meet two people you're attracted to. One finds you appealing, but the other doesn't. Which one is right?

The answer is neither of them. You just happen to fit one better than the other. It took me a long time to realize that certain types of people fit well together, and some don't. Most of successful dating is owning who you are then simply meeting enough people that you bump into someone who's a good fit.

One of my patients met a woman he thought was "the one." She didn't like him back—yet—but he thought he'd come across one of the only women he found attractive who *might* like him. He worked very hard to figure out how to earn her affection. He asked me what social skills to use, how to interact with her, and which sides of himself to accentuate. He worked himself into the ground trying to make it happen with this woman. But she was very clearly not super interested. She was a "maybe" at best, but not a solid "yes."

Then he met another woman who was a great fit and liked him. They had a ton of stuff in common, and they connected organically. She liked the things that naturally came out of his mouth and she found him attractive exactly as he was. He came in one session completely stunned. "There's a girl who's into me for who I am? I didn't think this was possible."

The more interactions you have, the more successful you'll be in dating. When you talk to more people, you'll interact with more potential good fits for you.

## Welcome to Affiliation Mode

Rejection is rough, but it's not the dramatically awful experience our threat system assumes it is. People tend to be surprisingly polite when they reject you. However, we can't help but have strong responses to rejection. Therefore, it's important to anticipate and respect our own internal pain.

With enough experience (and some active coping), rejection loses its sting over time, and therefore loses its ability to control your life. Although rejection feels like a failure in the moment, the real benefits are in the future. That's how it was for me and rejection month.

Almost immediately after my experiment had concluded so wonderfully with a woman laughing in my face in Harvard Square—and me not caring— I was sitting in a coffee shop. A girl sat on the couch alongside me and started reading. Her book looked interesting, and before I knew it, and without any planning or thought, I spontaneously asked her about it. She smiled and talked away about how much she loved the book.

Without realizing it, rejection month had propelled me into the Warm Social World. I was entering something I call "affiliation mode."

**CHAPTER 8 REFERENCES**

# Overcoming the Fear of Rejection

Exposure therapy summary

Abramowitz, J. S., Deacon, B. J., & Whiteside, S. P. H. (2019).
*Exposure therapy for anxiety: Principles and practice*
(2nd ed.). The Guilford Press.

## The Pain of Rejection and the Downward Spiral

Pain and self-esteem often drop after rejection

DeWall, C. N., & Bushman, B. J. (2011). Social acceptance and
rejection: The sweet and the bitter. *Current Directions in
Psychological Science, 20*(4), 256–260.

Smart Richman, L., & Leary, M. R. (2009). Reactions to
discrimination, stigmatization, ostracism, and other forms of
interpersonal rejection: A multimotive model. *Psychological
review, 116*(2), 365–383.

Rejection is physically painful

Eisenberger, N. I. (2013). Why rejection hurts: The
neuroscience of social pain. In C. N. DeWall (Ed.), *The
Oxford handbook of social exclusion* (pp. 152–162). Oxford
University Press.

Rejection by the KKK

Gonsalkorale, K., & Williams, K. (2007). The KKK won't let
me play: Ostracism even by a despised outgroup hurts.
*European Journal of Social Psychology, 37*(6), 1176-1186.

Fake rejection still hurts

Zadro, L., Williams, K., & Richardson, R. (2004). How low can
you go? Ostracism by a computer is sufficient to lower
self-reported levels of belonging, control, self-esteem,
and meaningful existence. *Journal of Experimental Social
Psychology, 40*(4), 560-567.

The impact of rejection on social behavior

Twenge, J. M., Catanese, K. R., & Baumeister, R. F. (2002). Social exclusion causes self-defeating behavior. *Journal of Personality and Social Psychology, 83*(3), 606–615.

Richman, L., & Leary, M. R. (2009). Reactions to discrimination, stigmatization, ostracism, and other forms of interpersonal rejection: A multimotive model. *Psychological review, 116*(2), 365–383.

Lonely people have a specific way of thinking

Cacioppo, J., & Hawkley, L. (2009). Perceived social isolation and cognition. *Trends in Cognitive Sciences, 13*(10), 447-454.

Why we're built to suffer in the face of rejection

Williams, K. D. (2001). Ostracism: The power of silence. Guilford Press.

Leary, M. R. (2007). *Interpersonal rejection.* New York: Oxford University Press.

Cacioppo, J. T., & Hawkley, L. C. (2009). Loneliness. In M. R. Leary & R. H. Hoyle (Eds.), *Handbook of Individual Differences in Social Behavior* (p. 227–240). The Guilford Press.

Heinrich, L. M., & Gullone, E. (2006). The clinical significance of loneliness: a literature review. *Clinical psychology review, 26*(6), 695–718.

Why we often shut down after rejection

Sloman, L., & Gilbert, P. (Eds.). (2000). Subordination and defeat: An evolutionary approach to mood disorders and their therapy. Lawrence Erlbaum Associates Publishers.

Sloman, L., Gilbert, P., & Hasey, G. (2003). Evolved mechanisms in depression: The role and interaction of attachment and social rank in depression. *Journal of Affective Disorders, 74*(2), 107–121.

## Most Rejections Are Polite

People are subtle and kind when they reject

Perper, T., & Weis, D. L. (1987). Proceptive and rejective strategies of U.S. and Canadian college women. *Journal of Sex Research, 23*(4), 455–480.

Goodboy, A.K., & Brann, M. (2010). Flirtation rejection strategies: Toward an understanding of communicative disinterest in flirting. *The Qualitative Report, 15,* 268-278.

Folkes, V. S. (1982). Communicating the reasons for social rejection. *Journal of Experimental Social Psychology, 18*(3), 235–252.

Women's rejections are so sweet and subtle that
the men don't take the hint in unrequited love

Baumeister, R. F., Wotman, S. R., & Stillwell, A. M. (1993). Unrequited love: On heartbreak, anger, guilt, scriptlessness, and humiliation. *Journal of Personality and Social Psychology, 64*(3), 377–394.

## The Internal Effects of Rejection

How rejection can affect us

Richman, L., & Leary, M. R. (2009). Reactions to discrimination, stigmatization, ostracism, and other forms of interpersonal rejection: A multimotive model. *Psychological review, 116*(2), 365–383.

Mallott, M. A., Maner, J. K., DeWall, N., & Schmidt, N. B. (2009). Compensatory deficits following rejection: The role of social anxiety in disrupting affiliative behavior. *Depression and Anxiety, 26*(5), 438–446.

DeWall, C. N., & Bushman, B. J. (2011). Social acceptance and rejection: The sweet and the bitter. *Current Directions in Psychological Science, 20*(4), 256–260.

## Coping with Rejection

Social support and coping

Baldwin, M. W., & Holmes, J. G. (1987). Salient private audiences and awareness of the self. *Journal of Personality and Social Psychology, 52*(6), 1087–1098.

Taylor, S. E. (2011). Social support: A review. In H. S. Friedman (Ed.), *The Oxford Handbook of Health Psychology* (pp. 189–214). Oxford University Press.

Heinrich, L. M., & Gullone, E. (2006). The clinical significance of loneliness: A literature review. *Clinical psychology review, 26*(6), 695–718.

The fundamental human needs to being

Baumeister, R. F., & Leary, M. R. (1995). The need to belong: Desire for interpersonal attachments as a fundamental human motivation. *Psychological Bulletin, 117*(3), 497–529.

Meditation and coping with rejection

Gyurak, A., & Ayduk, O. (2007). Defensive physiological reactions to rejection: The effect of self-esteem and attentional control on startle responses. *Psychological science, 18*(10), 886–892.

The coalition of single women

https://www.theonion.com/attractive-girls-union-refuses-to-enter-into-talks-with-1819594753

## Ending Your Abusive Relationship with Anxiety

The regret of not trying to date

Joel, S., Plaks, J. E., & MacDonald, G. (2019). Nothing ventured, nothing gained: People anticipate more regret from missed romantic opportunities than from rejection. *Journal of Social and Personal Relationships, 36*(1), 305–336.

## Rejection Exposure in the Real World

Exposure therapy summary

Abramowitz, J. S., Deacon, B. J., & Whiteside, S. P. H. (2019). *Exposure therapy for anxiety: Principles and practice* (2nd ed.). The Guilford Press.

Social snacking and shielding

Gardner, W. L., Pickett, C. L., & Knowles, M. (2005). Social snacking and shielding: Using social symbols, selves, and surrogates in the service of belonging needs. In K. D. Williams, J. P. Forgas, & W. von Hippel (Eds.), *The social outcast: Ostracism, social exclusion, rejection, and bullying* (pp. 227–241). Psychology Press.

Paravati, E., Naidu, E., & Gabriel, S. (2020). From "love actually" to love, actually: The sociometer takes every kind of fuel. *Self and Identity, 20*(1), 6-24.

Schäfer, K. & Eerola, T. (2020). How listening to music and engagement with other media provide a sense of belonging: An exploratory study of social surrogacy. *Psychology of Music, 48*(2), 232-251.

Exercise benefits for anxiety

Pontifex, M. B., Parks, A. C., Delli Paoli, A. G., Schroder, H. S., & Moser, J. S. (2021). The effect of acute exercise for reducing cognitive alterations associated with individuals high in anxiety. *International Journal of Psychophysiology: Official Journal of the International Organization of Psychophysiology, 167*, 47–56.

CHAPTER 9

. . .

# Welcome to the Warm Social World

I had a nice, quick, easy conversation with that girl in the coffee shop. No big fireworks, no phone number, no date. To an observer, it would have looked perfectly normal. But internally, something was very different.

Then I noticed it happen again. I was in a bar, and before I knew it I was talking to the girl next to me. Then it happened in other social situations—parties, in line at the grocery store, out to eat. I felt a natural urge to be warm towards someone I found attractive, then before I knew it I was interacting with them. It was organic and effortless.

My old analysis process was gone. I didn't think to myself, "Oh, I should talk to her. What should I say?" Instead, I was interacting without self-protection. My threat threshold had been pushed so far back that it no longer kicked in. I wasn't fighting against myself to be friendly, I was just being friendly. I wasn't suppressing my anxiety, I just wasn't experiencing it. And let me tell you: life was so much easier.

I used to regularly see women who looked like my type or seemed really cool, and I'd think, "I wish she was in my social circle so I could go talk to her." I was only able to meet people in a few low-stakes situations (at a house party, friend of a friend, etc.) and had no other options. But here's the thing: what if my ideal partner was sitting near me at a restaurant, in a bookstore, on the train, or walking down the street? No luck.

But after my exposure therapy in rejection month, this changed. I was no longer afraid of rejection like before, so I was no longer constrained by my old rules. I now realized I could talk to anybody.

I had entered the Warm Social World.

Let's be honest here: it's socially weird to walk up to a stranger on the street and talk to them. That's why rejection month resulted in so many rejections. Compared to a completely forced, unnatural conversation you'd get approaching a stranger on the street, a quick chat in a coffee shop (or other approved social environment) was easy.

The more I interacted with people in little moments throughout the day, the more positively they responded to me. Some of those quick interactions even became dates. If you expect to see warmth in the world, then you will. And remember: one positive interaction can more than make up for many rejections. It makes sense when you think about it. Consider the damage that one rejection causes. It's painful, sure, but compare it to the pleasure, self-esteem boost, and life-changing benefit of one positive connection (rejections are brief, but a positive connection can last the rest of your life). You don't need tons of people—or even two people—to be into you. You just need one. And one success here can make up for many rejections. In this chapter, we'll explore the frameworks and science to help you understand why the experience is so different on the other side of anxiety, and whether the payoffs I just mentioned are worth the pain of getting there.

## The Success Mindset

Have you ever experienced a mindset shift after

a really rewarding social interaction, especially with someone you found attractive? You feel a foot taller, you realize how attractive you've always been, everything around you looks so beautiful, and you feel friendly and eager to have great conversations with others. Everything feels easier because you just know people will respond well to you—and guess what? They do! The researchers Hawkley and Cacioppo put it nicely in a 2009 chapter:

"Whereas lonely individuals think about and behave towards others in a way that tends to reinforce an isolated existence, socially connected individuals hold a more favorable view of others that in turn tends to reinforce their being perceived and treated positively."

You walk around and see positive, happy people with a lot to offer. You're happy to go out and socialize, because you always end up meeting people, and you know you'll get along well. You don't feel threatened, and you aren't concerned about the potential impact of someone not liking you. You know you can talk to people you find attractive and some of them will like you. You don't feel socially threatened by anybody, you're proud of yourself, and you have genuine self-confidence. Over time, if you continue to live in this affiliative state, you'll date people you never would have believed could be interested in you. All the while, you'll do nothing specifically to make people like you. Friendliness will just ooze out of you, and connections will happen effortlessly.

This experience can be so wonderful, and so strikingly different from the anxiety that often consumes us, that I wanted to understand it.

I always wondered if there were treatment techniques that could get anyone into that mindset at any time. I experimented with different cognitive tactics, including remembering and talking about past successes, doing social warmups to get in the mood to chat, and so on. I even created a computer program that artificially flooded my emotional brain with acceptance images faster than my rational brain had time to dispute. All of it was wonderfully effective for about 20 minutes—then the effect would drop off. To be permanent, you need something deeper.

## GO KARTS AND THREAT AVOIDANCE

I was a nervous little kid the first time I ever went go-karting. In the middle of the race, someone had to pull me over and tell me not to press the accelerator and the brake at the same time. I wanted to drive fast, but I was scared. That's a lot like dating anxiety. In psychological terms we call it an approach-avoidance conflict: one part of you wants to approach a goal, but the other part of you is motivated to avoid a threat.

Think about how powerful your dating anxiety is, and the strength with which it can push you away from what you want. Now imagine a system equally as powerful in the opposite direction. When you stop practicing threat avoidance, watch out—once you take your foot off the brakes, who knows how quickly your life will accelerate into the Warm Social World.

In the presence of a stressor, your threat system takes over your body and cuts off your ability to connect. Your eyes don't function properly, your throat gets constricted, talking becomes difficult, and your body does everything it can to shut off the negative stimulation. These behaviors lead to you getting stuck in your own head, closing off to hide "flaws," trying to seem better than you are, and ultimately sending out signals of disconnection. Even if your goal is to connect, it's hard when you have to fight your own body.

The solution isn't to get better at fighting your body. It's teaching your body that there's no reason for self-protection at all. Once you follow the steps in this book to open yourself to connection, you'll discover what some researchers call the "social engagement system" underneath. Once there, you don't have to force social behaviors—they happen naturally. When your body doesn't feel like it's threatened, it organically and naturally opens and moves towards successful connection.

## Threat Mode vs. Affiliation Mode

Let's look at the difference between what I call threat mode and affiliation mode (Paul Gilbert calls this agonic and hedonic modes).

- Threat mode is the psychological regulation system we get pulled into in times of danger or threat. As you know, it gets activated when you're in socially threatening situations, and involves being acutely aware of status, resources, rivals, and other threats.
- On the other hand is affiliation mode. This refers to how you feel when you're around friends and people you like. You look around and see allies rather than rivals, you see people who might help you rather than challenge you. You connect easily and you talk freely. You socialize much better in this mode because you're built to operate in affiliation mode. All your systems

work together to facilitate this—your hormones, your neurotransmitters, your social motivation, the images your brain produces, your impulses, your facial expressions, and your body movements.

Depending on which mode you're in, you can experience the same situation in completely different ways.

Consider the good-natured teasing that is a staple of young male connection. Essentially, some aspects of masculinity make it hard for guys to be openly caring with each other, so it's often combined with mock aggression. I've noticed that friends who are in affiliation mode respond to teasing by smiling, laughing, and playing along. They seemingly understand this as a method of connection and a display of affection.

When you're in threat mode, however, male teasing can be seen as a devastating attack on our meager social status. The response? Quiet seething, clumsy lashing out, and escalating rebuttals that tend to trigger continued teasing.

One time at a party, I met a guy who I could tell was the most popular guy there, but he wasn't the center of attention. He was warm, friendly, and had fun with everybody. He enjoyed communicating, but he seemed just as happy to listen and laugh with somebody else if they happened to be in the spotlight. He didn't seem concerned with winning social points, but instead gave "points" away to others easily. This is the easy socializing that comes with affiliation mode.

While interacting in threat mode, people tend to be concerned with saying cool things, making good jokes, and making other people notice you. I remember complaining to my friends in college that they were making too many jokes around a girl I had a crush on—I was convinced they were scoring social points and making me look inferior by comparison!

In a competition mindset, resources are scarce and rivals plenty. As a result, you have to seize as much as you can, and fight off others who have the same goal. There can be only one winner in threat mode. You'll notice a lot of jealousy, complaining about people, and judging. Another friend in college did a ton of underhanded things to people, but he justified it by saying, "I know they'd do the same to me, I just did it first." He really believed that because he made it true in his worldview. He eventually created a world that lived up to his expectations.

## The Matthew Effect

Threat mode is a zero-sum game in which you can only get something by taking it away from others. However, in affiliation mode, resources and potential romantic partners are plentiful, and others tend to respond to you with love. Warmth and love are unlimited resources. If you're warm to somebody, they will more likely respond with warmth, which will make it easier for you to continue being friendly. Even more importantly, that person will feel good about themselves and pass that warmth on to other people they encounter. And you'll do the same.

In fact, one 2014 study found that even a small, pleasant social interaction with a coffee shop barista can make you feel happier, and improve your sense of belonging.

> You don't lose love by giving love, you just keep creating more of it.

Remember the quote: "Whatever you believe the world is withholding from you, you are actually withholding from the world." If you give love, affection, and attention to people, you're more likely to get that in return. When you're competitive and antagonistic, you likely trigger that same response in those around you.

This is known as the Matthew Effect: the rich get richer, and the poor get poorer.

This insight lines up with research into loneliness. The most social people end up thinking and behaving in ways that lead to more social connection. The more social interaction they have, the warmer they become, the more affiliative they feel, the better view they hold of others, the more they interact, the more they take social risks, the more social practice they get, the better connections they build. Therefore, those people with the most connections get more connections. In contrast, the loneliest people go through the direct opposite process, and end up being even lonelier.

## Lonely Cognitions

Lonely people tend to ruminate on thoughts that "other people are mean" and that "nobody will like me." These thoughts are referred to as lonely cognitions. As a result of lonely cognitions, lonely people fail to recognize when people are being open, friendly, and hoping for more connection. Instead, they see the world as a hotbed of rejection.

How inviting or uninviting the social world seems can be a matter of our thought process. I can remember multiple times when a girl smiled at me and I moved away from her rather than towards her, because I assumed she was smiling at somebody else. And if she was smiling at me, she would soon discover what a loser I was, I would screw it up, or worst of all, she was just playing a trick on me. I actually had a roommate in college tell me that the girl who accepted a date with me must be scamming me in some unexplained way, perhaps to make me buy things for her. The world is a pretty dreary place through that lens, isn't it?

Which leads me to a concept called behavioral confirmation. This refers to the phenomenon that people tend to behave the way we expect, such that they confirm our expectations. If we expect someone to be mean, then the way we approach them, our facial expressions, our voice tone, how open or closed off we are, or the types of questions we ask are very likely to elicit behavior that seems to confirm our expectations. Similarly, if you expect someone to be warm, you're more likely to interact with them in a way that elicits warmth.

I remember one night that demonstrated this concept to me. I was at a bar with my friend and we started talking to a woman. It was going well and she was friendly, then we decided to go back to our table. We bumped into her again 10 minutes later, and picked up right where we left off. We were friendly, she was friendly, and about five minutes into the conversation she said something that made it quite clear this was an entirely different person. Oops. We thought we knew her, so we expected her to be very friendly. We communicated with this stranger in such a way that we likely behaviorally confirmed her as friendly. Of course, maybe she was just a super friendly person and it would've happened anyway. But there is a lot of research showing that when people (even socially anxious people) are erroneously led to believe that a group is going to like them very much, they interacted in such a way that they were well received.

The point is, our social world is subjective, and when your social threat system is turned off, socializing is natural and easy, and that easiness tends to be reflected back to us.

## A Few Good Principles

It is possible to actually overcome dating anxiety. It's hard work, but I want you to realize the destination, the Warm Social World—is good enough to warrant it. You won't simply become better at pushing through discomfort. You'll enter a new place where socializing and dating becomes easy and natural. This is the land where the rich get richer, and you get all the rewards of health, happiness, and great relationships.

By the time I was in a consistent affiliation mode, I knew my life's work was helping other people get there too. I also knew I didn't want people to have to go through even 10% of what I did to get the rewards. I don't want you to have to memorize all the principles and theories every time you think about socializing. There's a lot of information in this book, and it's easy to get overwhelmed.

We know that the best goals are simple—so simple that we can remember them in times of stress. So in the conclusion, let's see if we can boil everything down to a few basic ideas that you can focus on when you're out in the dating world.

# Welcome to the Warm Social World

## The Success Mindset

How socially connected people think
Cacioppo, J. T., & Hawkley, L. C. (2009). Loneliness. In M.
  R. Leary & R. H. Hoyle (Eds.), Handbook of individual
  differences in social behavior (p. 227–240). The Guilford
  Press.

The social engagement system
Porges S. W. (2009). The polyvagal theory: New insights
  into adaptive reactions of the autonomic nervous system.
  Cleveland Clinic Journal of Medicine, 76 Suppl 2(Suppl 2),
  S86–S90.

## Threat Mode vs. Affiliation Mode

Articles regarding threat and affiliation
(agonic and hedonic) modes
Gilbert, P. (2001). Evolution and social anxiety: The role of
  attraction, social competition, and social hierarchies.
  Psychiatric Clinics of North America, 24(4), 723–751.

Gilbert, P., & Trower, P. (1990). The evolution and manifestation
  of social anxiety. In W. R. Crozier (Ed.), Shyness and
  embarrassment: Perspectives from social psychology (pp.
  144–177). Cambridge University Press.

## The Matthew Effect

Evidence of the virtuous circle in which
positivity builds positivity
Trew, J., & Alden, L. (2015). Kindness reduces avoidance goals
  in socially anxious individuals. Motivation and Emotion,
  39(9), 892-907.

Alden, L., & Trew, J. (2013). If it makes you happy: Engaging in kind acts increases positive affect in socially anxious individuals. *Emotion, 13*(1), 64-75.

Sloman, L., & Dunham, D. W. (2004). The Matthew effect: Evolutionary implications. *Evolutionary Psychology, 2,* 92–102.

Sandstrom, G. M., & Dunn, E. W. (2014). Social interactions and well-being: The surprising power of weak ties. *Personality and Social Psychology Bulletin, 40*(7), 910–922.

Sandstrom, G. M., & Dunn, E. W. (2014). Is efficiency overrated?: Minimal social interactions lead to belonging and positive affect. *Social Psychological and Personality Science, 5*(4), 437–442.

## Lonely Cognitions

Lonely people have a specific way of thinking
Cacioppo, J. T., & Hawkley, L. C. (2009). Loneliness. In M. R. Leary & R. H. Hoyle (Eds.), Handbook of individual differences in social behavior (p. 227–240). The Guilford Press.

The upward spiral of confirmation
Curtis, R. C., & Miller, K. (1986). Believing another likes or dislikes you: Behaviors making the beliefs come true. *Journal of Personality and Social Psychology, 51*(2), 284–290.

Behavioral confirmation studies
Smith-Genthôs, K. R., Reich, D. A., Lakin, J. L., & Casa de Calvo, M. P. (2015). The tongue-tied chameleon: The role of nonconscious mimicry in the behavioral confirmation process. *Journal of Experimental Social Psychology, 56,* 179–182.

Snyder, M., & Klein, O. (2005). Construing and constructing others: On the reality and the generality of the behavioral confirmation scenario. *Interaction Studies: Social Behaviour and Communication in Biological and Artificial Systems, 6*(1), 53–67.

If we expect acceptance, we are warm
and we receive acceptance

Stinson, D.A., Cameron, J.J., Wood, J.V., Gaucher, D., & Holmes, J.G. (2009). Deconstructing the "reign of error": Interpersonal warmth explains the self-fulfilling prophecy of anticipated acceptance. *Personality and Social Psychology Bulletin, 35*(9), 1165-1178.

CONCLUSION

. . .

# The Power of Pro-Social Risks

Dating anxiety isn't a problem. It's an ancient evolutionary attempt to solve the problem of rejection. When triggered, we're compelled to anticipate and prevent rejection through a series of safety mechanisms—what I referred to throughout the book as threat mode. While this may have been useful in our caveman past, in the modern world it's counterproductive. Our protective mechanisms make rejection more likely, cut off any chance of connection, and reinforce our anxiety. Now that you've dropped your protective armor, and taught your system that you don't need it to protect you, you're free to show more of yourself, and risk being seen for who you are.

You're flawed, and you are still worthy of love. We can now see that the anxiety equation just doesn't hold up:

1. Your perceived flaws may not be revealed
2. They may not be obvious or people might not notice them
3. Maybe they won't consider them flaws, but rather quirks (or even something cute)
4. Maybe they are accepting or kind, not judgmental of imperfections
5. Maybe they see you as a whole person, and understand everyone has flaws
6. If you aren't a fit with someone, maybe you can tolerate that and cope

But now what?

It's hard to absorb an entire book. I usually find that by the time I've finished a book, I've already forgotten all of its ideas. Let's take a quick look back, review the information we covered, and translate it into a simple, elegant plan for low anxiety dating.

## Your Low Anxiety Dating Plan

The core of my dating plan philosophy boils down to two questions:

- Who are you?
- What are you looking for?

I know it sounds simple, but these questions cut deep. When I ask clients these questions, most of the time people have little to no idea. Why? Research has found that people with social anxiety have reduced self-concept clarity. This is a fancy way of saying they don't know with certainty and consistency who they are, and are therefore lacking in conviction. Thus they are less likely to act in line with their views. Knowing who you are and acting in accordance with it is very attractive in dating and social life. Acting faithfully to yourself is the definition of self-confidence.

It's totally expected to not know the answer to the question "Who are you?" You have to experiment, observe yourself, and learn along the way.

One 2011 study found that simply asking yourself to define your most important values and why they matter is enough to reduce social anxiety and improve social skills. To better articulate who you are, ask yourself the following questions:

- What is it about you that makes you great to date? We all have traits that make us a good partner—what are yours?
- What are some compliments you've gotten from people? If you can't think of any, ask some trusted family members and friends what they see as your best traits.
- What do you stand for?
- What matters to you most in your life?
- What do you think is important and what doesn't matter as much to you as it does to others?

If you answer those questions with deep honesty, you'll have a good idea of who you are. Then, once you've done that, your next step is to articulate what you're looking for. Being authentically choosy and having standards in dating is attractive. Similarly, not having standards is unattractive. It's also a terrible idea in general for you to date people you don't fit with. To that end, answer the following questions:

- What kind of relationship do I want right now?
- How do I need to be treated by a partner?
- What traits do I want in a partner?
- What traits do I want to avoid in a partner?
- What are red flags and deal-breakers I want to watch for, and why?

Then (and here comes the harder part) you need to act in alignment with these answers. You need to be willing to own who you are and who you're looking for, regardless of whether it's going to bring you acceptance or rejection. Let me make this blatant:

Own who you are even if you think the person you're attracted to will dislike you for it. If getting acceptance from someone requires ignoring one of your standards or values, that person isn't for you.

Obviously be reasonable about it all—there's room to experiment and explore your boundaries. Don't use this as a subtle safety behavior to avoid trying to connect with people: "I said I preferred blue eyes, so I'm not going talk to that green-eyed person over there."

With the foundation of your dating plan in place, it's time to take action:

- Go out and socialize with people regularly. If you're in group situations, try to introduce yourself to 3 new people each time. Don't perform, just let your impression take care of itself.
- No worrying before socializing and no rumination afterwards.
- Focus externally on other people and be genuinely curious. *What's interesting about this person? What do I like about this person?*
- Listen to their answers to your questions, and seek to truly understand them.
- When ideas come naturally to your mind, share them without filtering beyond the blatantly obscene.
- Ask the questions that pop up naturally, share your reactions and stories that you think of spontaneously.
- Just as you want to find out who this other person really is, allow them to

discover who you are in the moment, flaws and all.

- Own who you are—own your interests, own your quirks, own your flaws, and own your strengths. Then see where it goes.
- If you are attracted, allow that to be naturally expressed through your body language and your desire to invest your time and attention.
- When there's not a fit, chalk it up as an exposure victory, practice active coping, and continue.

Boom, there it is—your low anxiety dating plan. Remember: dating isn't a battle or a sales call. It's a voyage of discovery. So let your freak flag fly, and see where the river takes you. You never know what's around the next bend. Maybe you're a fit with someone you don't expect. Maybe someone you really like at first turns out to be a terrible fit. Either way, enjoy your interactions and keep moving through discomfort. No matter what, keep socializing—again, and again, and again.

There's a Warm Social World out there waiting for you, if you're open enough to discover it. You now have the framework to understand it, and the tools to move out of threat mode and into affiliation mode. I hope this book has been helpful for you. But now you must move from ideas into experience. The emotional system only learns through doing. So I'll leave you with one last idea.

People are just like you. People are good, people want to be kind, people want to be respected, people crave authenticity, and people want to be seen and accepted for who they are. So go out and meet some of them. There's no end to the fun and excitement you'll experience if you do.

CONCLUSION REFERENCES

# The Power of Pro-Social Risks
The problem of not knowing who you
are and what matters to you

R

Orr, E. M. J., & Moscovitch, D. A. (2015). Blending in at the cost of losing oneself: Dishonest self-disclosure erodes self-concept clarity in social anxiety. *Journal of Experimental Psychopathology, 6*(3), 278–296.

Stinson, D. A., Logel, C., Shepherd, S., & Zanna, M. P. (2011). Rewriting the self-fulfilling prophecy of social rejection: Self-affirmation improves relational security and social behavior up to 2 months later. *Psychological Science, 22*(9), 1145–1149.

THE POWER OF PRO-SOCIAL RISKS · 333

. . .

# Acknowledgments

I've been working on some version of this book since before I had any right to be, back when I was just a young anxious guy sitting in coffee shops discovering fascinating research ideas, and doing silly behavioral experiments in bars that no longer exist.

I truly wasn't sure I would ever finish or publish this book. And the fact that you are now holding it in your hands is due to the help of the following people:

Thanks to Greg Larson, my tireless editor, for taking a rambling, unorganized, repetitive tome and helping craft it down to something readable.

I'm eternally grateful to Jesse Sussman and Hope Needles for their invaluable support both professionally and (especially) personally in creating the book and audiobook.

Thanks to Kain Warwick, Ben Freda, Stan Taylor, and Josef Kannegaard for contributing in multiple ways over many years. I have great appreciation also for Drs. Diana Damer, Marianne Stout, and Peter Vernig for helping me to learn and develop an understanding of social and dating anxiety treatment.

Finally, thanks to my parents—Margot and Tony Smithyman—for all their support and encouragement, not just with this book but with my entire journey.

I'm very happy to finish this, and, even more than that, I feel fantastically lucky to do so with a wonderful group of people. Your importance to me can't be understated. Thank you again.

# About the Author

Dr. Thomas Smithyman is a clinical psychologist who specializes in treating social anxiety and other anxiety disorders. He has a Ph.D. in Clinical Psychology from Suffolk University, where he also served as an adjunct professor. Dr. Smithyman co-hosts the Anxious in Austin podcast and creates psychoeducational videos on YouTube to help others overcome social anxiety and form genuine connections.

Outside of his career, Thomas is a songwriter and performer, and has a lifelong goal of becoming fluent in Italian.

If you'd like to receive more resources and information about overcoming social anxiety, sign up for Thomas's newsletter at *thomassmithyman.com/subscribe*.

Printed in Great Britain
by Amazon